would you like

with that?

At the age of 25 Justin was sick of constantly falling short of his goals, so he decided to take control of his life and use his last $50 to start his own business. With no prior experience behind him, he had to learn quickly to survive and, eventually, to thrive in the business world. Several years on—and a lot of hard work and determination later—Attitude Inc.® is now a multimillion-dollar company, and Justin, at the age of 32, has retired from the everyday running of the business. Justin is now free to pursue his latest challenges—public speaking and writing—as well as the many other business ventures he no doubt has up his sleeve! And yes, he did manage to buy the car of his dreams . . .

would you like

with that?

justin herald

NO LIMITS, NO EXCUSES,
NO IFS, NO BUTS ... JUST ATTITUDE

ALLEN&UNWIN

First published in 2003

Allen & Unwin
83 Alexander Street
Crows Nest NSW 2065
Australia
Phone: (61 2) 8425 0100
Fax: (61 2) 9906 2218
Email: info@allenandunwin.com
Web: www.allenandunwin.com

National Library of Australia
Cataloguing-in-Publication entry:

Herald, Justin.
    Would you like attitude with that? no limits, no excuses, no ifs,
    no buts . . . just attitude.

    ISBN 1 74114 057 9.

    1. Success. 2. Self-realisation. I. Title.

158.1

Text design by Tabitha King
Set in 10/14 pt Sabon by Midland Typesetters, Maryborough, Victoria
Printed in Australia by McPherson's Printing Group

10 9 8 7 6 5 4 3

This book is dedicated to
my three favourite
girls in the world.

Vanessa: Thank you for putting up with me over the
years and for believing in me.
Jade: For being my reality check and keeping
me laughing every day.
Brooke: For just being you.

contents

introduction

IT'S NOT WHETHER YOU GET KNOCKED DOWN...IT'S WHETHER YOU GET UP

© Attitude Inc.®

The whole purpose of this book is to show you how you can change your view, your thinking and your actions, to get them back on track towards achieving those goals you set years ago and those dreams you have always wanted to become reality. I don't want to just tell you all of the good things that have happened to me over the last seven years of my business life, however, as I believe that would be unrealistic.

To be honest, it has been a hard slog, with many many disappointments as well as successes. I want to share some of those disappointments with you so you have some practical examples to compare with your own situations. I also want to show you how, if and when you apply some of the principles from these experiences, you can accelerate your progress and journey.

We all go through life wanting more for ourselves, striving to be better and trying to reach greater heights. The problem is that many of us, myself included, fall short at times of actually reaching those heights, and then become disillusioned with our goals and dreams. We may even give up entirely, and stop applying ourselves to achieving what we had set out to do.

Throughout this book, I will highlight what I believe are the keys to getting back on track and getting re-focused on those outcomes you set out to achieve months and maybe even years ago.

In the last seven years since starting my business, Attitude Inc.®, I have been asked many times what exactly my secret was in taking $50 to a national, and now international, brand. I can honestly say that the keys and principles that you are about to read are the 'secret to my success'.

There is absolutely no difference between you and me. We all shower the same, get dressed the same, even probably eat the same. Anyone who tries to exalt themself over others is really only cheating themself and those around them.

If nothing changes, nothing changes

Here is the first principle I adapted to my situation. I used my frustration with where my life was at and where it was headed seven years ago, and channelled that frustration towards making a permanent change in my life.

DON'T BE SCARED OF CHANGE, AS MOST TIMES CHANGE WILL BRING ABOUT RELEASE

If you apply this principle to your life, I can guarantee that not only will you have a brighter outlook on those goals and dreams you have set yourself, you will also be able to move closer to achieving them.

Sick and tired of facing the same situations and the same frustrations every day, week and year, I decided on 2 February 1995 that I was going to try something different. I was going to take charge of my life and show not only those around me, but myself also, what I could do if I actually changed my thinking and actions.

Many of us get stuck trying to reach the goals that we have set ourselves. Sometimes we struggle for years and years. While you may not reach your goals overnight the journey can be made a lot easier and less painful if only we know what's involved.

Have a look at those around you—your work colleagues, your friends, and maybe even your family. How many of them are living their dreams and have reached their own personal goals? The answer for most of us will be, 'Only a few'. So you see, you and I are really no different to everyone else around us, but you can set yourself apart from those work colleagues, friends and family members if only you know how.

As you read on, you will see that I do not believe in failure. You can plateau at times, but as long as you try—and I mean really put your heart, soul and effort into reaching your desired outcomes—you will never 'fail'.

That doesn't mean that you will achieve everything that you set out to do all the time, but it does mean that the decisions you make, as long as you learn from the lessons along the way, will take you down the right path instead of one that is either going nowhere or in the totally opposite direction to where you originally wanted to go.

Don't be bitter, be better

You may have already made up your mind that this book is not really for you. You may have tried to reach those goals and dreams, but due to unforeseen circumstances you have fallen a bit short.

You have read all the books, listened to all the self-help tapes, maybe even attended some of the seminars on this issue, and still be nowhere close to those goals. Someone else's actions may have resulted in you going backwards in your journey; you may have been let down by those you thought had only your best interests in mind. We all have. It is what you learn from those experiences that will ultimately be the key to pushing through those mental barriers you have set up and which will ultimately translate into your actions.

Don't sit there for the rest of your life being bitter. Bitterness will only eat away at you like a grub on a leaf. You need to resolve, right now, that you will leave your thoughts open to being challenged by a different and maybe entirely new way of approaching your situation.

NEGATIVE THOUGHTS BRING NEGATIVE OUTCOMES

If you start seeing everything that has happened in the past, what is happening to you right now and what is going to happen to you in the future, as opportunities for change, you will overcome one of the most important barriers to changing your direction.

That 'stuff' that you have hung onto over the years—the

negative thinking, the mentality that what goes wrong is everybody else's fault, that your actions were misguided—needs to be addressed now. You need to commit yourself to spring cleaning all the negative stuff out of your mind and away from around you.

Don't play the victim game

You probably know people who do this—you probably work or associate with them every day. You know the type: they blame everyone and everything for the reason they are who they are, and where they are in life.

Having a victim mentality will only crush your desire to excel in your life. Blaming others is no way to overcome your problems. It may seem an easy way to hide those issues that you have been hanging onto for years, but it won't actually change them. You need to take control and move on with your pursuit of all that you want out of life.

Be a control freak when it comes to reaching your goals. Don't allow yourself to be swayed away from their completion. Just like the child who keeps a firm hold on their lollies, be the same with your dreams. Guard them against being taken away from your grasp. The biggest threat to them could be your own thoughts and actions.

Passion

Are you passionate about achieving your goals and dreams? Then you will need to use that same passion in the actual working towards those goals and dreams. You need to take that 'feeling' of passion and turn it into 'action' fuelled by that passion.

The subject of passion would have to be one of my most favourite things to talk about. Why is it that some people are just wired to succeed? We all know people around us who are so passionate, so enthusiastic about life, about their jobs and about everything they do, that they seem to be on a high all the time.

You see, those people have mastered one factor in reaching their goals—it is utilising their passion which makes them tick and function. It is this passion that we all need to adapt to our situations.

I can't stand wishy-washy people who just take whatever comes their way; they don't seem to get excited about anything. We need to charge into our lives and towards our goals and dreams with passion. Without passion, excitement and enthusiasm, we will either fall short of our expected outcome or not enjoy where we end up. With passion in your life, your focus will always stay straight.

PASSION IS WHY WE DO WHAT WE DO AND HOW WELL WE DO IT

Everyone can achieve something. It is how well, how passionately, you do it that relates to how great the reward is at the end. There is no point in having goals and dreams if you really don't care if you reach them.

Your goals and dreams need to consume your thinking and actions. They need to be a part of who you are—not in such a way that you become a freak while trying to achieve them, but you need to be driven by them. How passionate are you when it comes to achieving your goals? Do you care?

If you have just answered 'no' to this question, then you might as well put this book down, go to the beach and concentrate on your tan—but you could also decide to take back control of your situation, to not be a bystander for the rest of your life.

I would like to challenge you about your everyday situation, and maybe even point you towards some areas that you can work on.

This book is intended for those who own their own business, who are employed by someone, who are looking for a job, or who want to excel in their working and personal lives. Everybody really!

I have had many different business ideas over the years since I started Attitude Inc.®. It amazes even me how excited and, I think, passionate I can get about a new idea for a business. After a few hours or days, however, reality sets in—the hard work that will be needed, the finance needed to start, and so on.

When it comes to a business idea, it is very easy to get so caught up in the excitement of where you want to end up that the reality of getting there takes a back seat. You really have to remember that owning a business requires a lot of hard work and effort. The excitement will probably wear off pretty quickly.

We are all moved by emotions, and I talk about this in more detail later on. But never let those emotions rule your decisions in your business. I don't see passion as an emotion. Passion to me should be a lifestyle—when you are passionate about something, whether it is your business, your hobby or even your sport, it should colour every part of your thinking, your actions, your life. It is that passion that needs to be understood and fine tuned so that you can get the most out of what you are trying to achieve.

YOUR PASSION TOWARDS YOUR BUSINESS NEEDS TO BE YOUR GUIDE

The degree of passion that you have towards your business or job will dictate where your business or employment will peak. By that, I mean it is very easy to see why some businesses fail to achieve what the owner wants—there is no passion in what they are doing. If you just want a job, then don't own a business. Being a business owner requires first, a lot of skill and second, and most importantly, a lot of passion.

The passion that you have for your business will show in the results. There is no getting away from passion. You can't just turn up and expect everything to happen, that the business will excel. You need to apply passion and turn it into a tangible asset.

So sit down, grab a coffee or a tea, or something stronger, and relax and enjoy the journey. Be aware though, that if you are not prepared to make some changes—and they may only need to be small—then you may end up in the same position and feel the same way you did before you read this book. Remember—be passionate about achieving all that you want out of life.

GO HARD OR JUST GO HOME

© Attitude Inc.®

attitude

We all want good results out of our lives, whether it's our business, family or personal life. There is just one single word that will determine how well we succeed in these areas— *attitude*.

This word means a great deal to me, for two reasons:

1. It is how I live my life. My attitude has been the factor behind my greatest successes and my biggest regrets.
2. Attitude Inc.® is the company I founded in 1995, which we will touch on later in this chapter.

The attitude you have towards life now will determine where your life will end up. Have you ever met someone who is struggling with the day-to-day issues of their life? The longer you spend with them, the easier it is to see why they are in a particular position. They are a product of their own thinking and attitudes.

The word 'attitude' seems to be the buzzword these days. You hear it everywhere, in newspapers, on television, even at sports grounds. What does attitude really mean, and how do we change our attitude to help us achieve all we want out of life?

What I mean by attitude is: the position or direction that indicates your actions, feelings or moods. It is those actions, feelings and moods that direct us towards our life's goals. If you take a negative approach to life, and in turn have negative feelings and moods, your outcome will be negative. If you take a positive approach to life, and in turn have positive feelings and moods, your outcome will be positive. I know this sounds easy, but that is the point. It really is that easy.

Most people underestimate the damage they themselves do to what they want out of life by continually talking themselves down. It is hard enough sometimes getting through life with those around you being negative, but when you start to do it to yourself then things just shoot off in the wrong direction. It is attitude that lets everyone around us know what we are really like.

YOU CHOOSE. WHAT WOULD YOU RATHER BE AROUND? NEGATIVE OR POSITIVE?

I cannot stand being around negative people. Their attitude tries to bring everyone around them down to their level—and most of the time they are completely unaware of what they are doing. That is why I surround myself with positive, big-thinking people. The same principle applies—their attitude gives off a positive feeling. It is their attitude that is contagious; you can't help but be caught up in their mood.

I believe your attitude is like a mirror. The attitude you give out is the same attitude you will get back. Let me explain. Imagine going into a coffee shop. You sit down and you wait to place your order. The waitress comes to your table and says, 'Yeah, what do you want?' What she's really saying is, 'Hurry up, I'm not in a good mood.' Now I'm not sure about you, but that kind of attitude on her part will evoke a particular response from me. She has set the mood. No matter how hard you try, as long as she stays with this type of bad attitude, you may eventually give her back a little of what she is giving out—she has had an effect on your mood.

Her attitude is basically a mirror. She should not be surprised to receive the same treatment back. The problem is that when, not if, someone gives her a bit of attitude in return, she will most probably be taken aback and start complaining about 'all the rude people in the world today'. But if she comes to the table happy, helpful and willing to serve you, your response to her will also be cheerful.

You control your attitude

What attitude are you giving off to your friends, work colleagues or clients? Are you constantly having problems in your relationships with these people? If you are, you need to check your attitude. It is too easy to blame others for the way we are. Some of what you may be going through may be because of others, but I can guarantee that they are not there to change your outlook on life and your attitude. It is called 'your attitude' for a reason. It is *yours*!

Your attitude is something that you can control. Everyone you come in contact with on a daily basis will reflect back to you the attitude you present to them. So you see, ultimately it is our own attitude towards life that determines life's attitude towards us. It is the old cause and effect rule.

Everything that we say or do ultimately causes a corresponding effect. For every action there is a corresponding and equal reaction. If you are miserable with your life, those around you will reflect that outlook. They will gladly dump all their negativity on you, because this is what you are inviting. You will get to the end of the week drained of all life and miserable because you have allowed other people's negativity to be shovelled your way. On the other hand, if you love life, want the best out of life, and project that attitude, those around you will respond with positive inputs. You will have people around you building you up and wanting only the best for you. Your outlook on life will be one of positivity and excitement for what is to come.

Let me make it even simpler:

GREAT ATTITUDE—GREAT RESULT
GOOD ATTITUDE—GOOD RESULT
AVERAGE ATTITUDE—AVERAGE RESULT
POOR/BAD ATTITUDE—POOR/BAD RESULT

As you can see, *you* are the one responsible for your life. You get back into your life what you originally put out.

You can't expect everything to go your way if you are giving out negativity all the time. If you are reading this chapter, and you want to achieve more in your life, then you can. All you need to do is change your attitude. Until you change your attitude, nothing will change around you.

Let me put this concept in focus. Imagine sitting in front of an empty fireplace waiting for it to warm up. It is not going to warm up by itself. You need to put the wood in it and light it before the heat will come. The same theory applies in your own life. You need to start changing before the issues and people around you will change. It is no good waiting for people around you to change; even if they change, if you have done nothing you will still be the same you. It is too easy to think, 'If only they changed, everything would be all right.' While that's a lovely thought, the reality is that you will still have the same issues and problems you have always had; only the people around you are different. It is your life, your dreams and your goals; you are the captain of your own destiny. It just depends on where you want to steer your ship.

Most of us never consider where our attitude is on a daily basis. We get up in the morning with our attitude in neutral. We programme ourselves to adjust our attitude as the day goes on. The problem with doing this is that we are letting our circumstances rule our direction, or we are waiting for those around us to let us know where our attitude is at. It isn't until we get feedback about our attitude (and most of the time it isn't positive feedback) that we realise we need to check it. I don't know about you, but I want to be the con-troller of my life.

At the age of 25, I was sick and tired of going nowhere—and I was going nowhere because I was just handling what was dealt out to me. I was going with the flow, whatever life dished out, and I took it from there.

Many of us go through this same process every day. If only we could see that our attitude is the key to what comes our way, our direction would be a lot clearer. We have to be determined that nothing will inhibit our thinking, because it is our thought process that really directs us in our journey towards our goals and dreams.

My daughter Jade at the time of writing this book is in Year 5. She is constantly bringing home homework that I must say even tests me. From time to time when she is faced with a question she does not understand, Jade will come out with the old excuse 'I can't do that one'. You know, she is 100 per cent right. As long as she thinks she can't, she will not progress past that question and in return, learn something new.

I have a rule in my house. There is no such word as 'can't'. I have running arguments with Jade as she tries to prove that because the dictionary has 'can't' in it, it's a word that she can apply. But I tell her that as long as you give yourself the excuse that you can't do something, you will never be able to complete it, neither in your thinking nor in reality.

How many times have you been faced with a problem that seems too big to overcome? Do you give up even before you try? Who decides you can't overcome a problem? You certainly never will while you think like that. You have programmed your thinking to give up before you even start.

Have a look at successful people. Everything they seem to do is successful. Even when something doesn't work out the way they planned, they don't seem to get worried. They just move on to the next thing and become successful at that. Is this just luck? No! It is their attitude. It is not that they are smarter than the rest of us; they have just programmed their thinking and their attitude that nothing is going to stop them from succeeding. They expect to succeed. That is the key to what sets them apart from the rest, from those who would just give up or try something a little easier.

I have a friend who has tried every business under the sun and, I must say, has not done too well at any of them. Time and time again, he is telling me of a new venture. As time progresses, each new venture he gets involved in starts to go bad. Why is it that he is failing to succeed? Is it lack of funds? Maybe. Is it that no one sees his vision? Also maybe. But I think it is his attitude more than anything else that is the reason he is falling short of his goals. He is constantly blaming this person or that person for his ventures going under. Blame is a great way to hide your shortcomings. The minute he starts something new he is already waiting for it to come undone. He takes with him all the negative baggage from the time before and the time before that and so on. He has never dealt with the issues and attitudes he faced years ago. Until he changes his attitude and thinking, he will keep going around the same roundabout. Unfortunately, he is expecting to fail before he even starts.

It would be impossible to estimate the jobs lost, marriages ended, exams failed and friendships broken purely because of bad attitudes. What a shame. While we blame circumstances around us we never look to ourselves as the cause. After a while you will eventually run out of people to blame. Or will you?

It is time spent assessing our own bad attitudes and faults that will in the end be time well spent. We are all guilty of waiting for the world to change for us, fit in with us and operate by our guidelines and rules. That is great if our attitude is positive, but what if it is not. We will never be happy with anything we are given.

I know some people who, if they won $1 million in the lottery, would complain that the money was too heavy to carry home. We all know people like that, the same people who complain that nothing ever goes their way. It never will while their attitude towards life stinks. Their situations are a direct reflection of themselves.

We all need to be in control of our own circumstances—so, how do we change our attitude? If you want to have a positive outlook on life, you must first change your attitude to a positive one. If you want to be successful in life, you must first change your attitude to a successful one.

Until you change your attitude, your situation may change but it will only be for a short time as it is just surface change. The real changes we need to make are the deep-rooted issues that we have been carrying for a long time.

I am a really bad home handyman. Recently I had to paint a few walls around the house. I looked at the task before me and decided to do it the easy way (I'm not a great one for preparation when it comes to household chores). So I did what seemed a good idea at the time. I just painted over the old paint, as it was the same colour. The problem was that a few weeks later you could see the bad job I had done—the old paint surface was showing through the new paint. I should have sanded back the old paint, used an undercoat and then put the fresh paint on. Sanding requires a lot of time and effort. You need to put your whole body into it. The undercoat needs to be applied perfectly and with care, so the whole wall is covered evenly. Then you need to wait until the undercoat dries. Then, for perfection, the final coat needs to be painted on properly.

This analogy illustrates how some of us go through life. We do not spend time properly preparing ourselves for change. We just decide we are going to change without sanding back the bad things about ourselves. Further down the path, the issues that we didn't deal with weeks, months and even years previously, will inevitably pop up again. Addressing these issues should be a priority if you really want to achieve those goals and dreams that you have set for yourself.

DON'T PUT CHANGE OFF FOR ANOTHER DAY, DO IT NOW, DO IT TODAY!

If you are at a point where you have decided that you want more out of life, or you really want to change who you are, you need to firstly check out your attitude.

The Attitude Gear® story

My attitude towards life goes back to when I was young. All I wanted to do was do well at whatever I did. My business was formed out of having some people constantly telling me I had an 'attitude problem'. I didn't think I had one. Sure, I can be blunt sometimes, but all I knew was that I wanted to succeed in life and I was sick and tired of people getting in the way with their negative thinking and direction.

My father is a Christian minister. Throughout my childhood and adolescence I was constantly given other people's opinions as to how a minister's son should live. Most of the time I was told what I should do, and given advice and direction by people who were less than successful in their own lives. Go figure! After leaving high school at the age of 16 with less than good results (I think the only thing I passed was lunchtime and recess), I had many jobs. I did not know what I wanted to do.

Growing up in a minister's home, while I do not regret it one bit, was hard. So many people in the church seemed to think they could force on me their opinions about what I should be doing, who I was and what I was doing wrong. The problem was that when I looked at the people telling me these things, their lives were nowhere near perfect either.

In February 1995, a woman in the church I was attending decided to tell me everything that was wrong about me. At the end of her rather long-winded telling-off, she said the five words that have led me to where I am today: 'You have an attitude problem.' She finished up saying that unless I did something with this problem I would not go very far in life.

So I did what any 25-year-old would do: I decided to show her up. Being full of sarcasm and fed up with being judged incorrectly, I figured I could combine the two and take over the world. Well, that was my plan that day anyway.

Having worked for a few different companies and come up with what I thought were great ideas, only to see them rejected or taken and used with someone else getting the praise, I decided it was time for me to put up or shut up. With only $50 in my pocket, my business plan was simple: make a few shirts with 'Attitude' on them and upset as many people as I could, then go back to a real job.

Purchasing four blank t-shirts ran me out of money, but I was not going to let a minor detail called 'lack of working capital' stop me just yet. I approached a local printer. I sold him my dream. I spent two hours showing him how this new product, which I hadn't even got off the ground yet, was going to be the biggest thing since sliced bread.

I was on a roll. I could see the excitement coming from this man. Then I asked the most important question: 'Can you print these shirts for free?' To my surprise, he agreed, as long as I used him to print the future shirts. It was a done deal.

A few days later, I had four t-shirts with the Attitude logo across the front and the slogan 'In the end it's all a matter of Attitude' printed on the back. My plan was going well. Now it was time to show the woman at church what I was doing with my attitude problem.

The next Sunday I sold three of the shirts to three of my friends. Wearing the shirts, the four of us sat in the front row of the church in clear sight of the woman who days earlier had torn me to shreds. I was inundated that morning by people wanting to buy Attitude t-shirts. With the money I made from selling the three shirts I had enough capital to double my initial stock. I had another eight shirts made up, sold those, made another 16, then 32, then 64, and so on. I was well and truly on my way to owning my own business.

You see, it was my attitude that kept me focused. If I'd had the attitude that when I ran out of money buying the blank t-shirts it was all over, then it would have been. Over! But I was determined that I would control the situation around me. By thinking like that I was able to push through the problems I faced and adjust my thinking that I would be able to overcome future problems as well.

After many months of selling directly to people I knew, I had enough stock to sell to a retail outlet. The problem I had then was that none of the stores I approached wanted to take my brand on. Time and again I was told that no one was asking for Attitude Gear®, so they wouldn't stock it. I still think this is a very blinkered way of running a retail store. It's the chicken and the egg theory: how can people ask for the brand if they cannot see it? I decided I would have to think a bit laterally. I got a few of my mates together and came up with a plan: we would each ring a store and ask if they had any Attitude Gear®. Over a three-week period we all made calls to the same store. After that I would walk into the store and ask if they had heard of Attitude Gear®, and whether they would like to look at the range.

The response was unbelievable. Every time I walked into the stores we had been targeting, I was met with the same response. They ordered the stock on the spot, because they had been asked for it so many times. I created my own demand.

Once the stock went on the shelves, it sold out in record time. I had changed the shop-owners' thinking by using the method they would understand. Demand.

Within the first year of establishing Attitude Gear®, we had 60 stores across Australia carrying the brand, and it was selling well. Even so, I was still coming in contact with negative responses from less-than-business-minded retailers. I decided to prove once and for all that the public liked Attitude Gear®. I set up a stall in a local Sydney market, a place that attracted thousands of shoppers every weekend. In the first weekend at my market stall, I sold out of stock—selling around 200 shirts and 150 hats in total. Now I was certain the public liked the brand. This was the kick-start I needed. I was on a roll.

When I received negative feedback after this, I just let it bounce off me, because I knew I had a product that was going to do well. I was not going to let other people's misguided opinions dictate my future. My attitude was the factor in my positive outlook. Sure, I could have listened to the negativity coming from some of the retailers' mouths, but then I would have been operating on their level and my business would not have proceeded past the first week.

During the first three years, I had a part-time job as well to bring in extra capital. I was determined that I was going to give my business the best possible chance to succeed, no matter what the personal cost, and Attitude Gear® grew about 100–150 per cent each of those years.

Most of the time as the business took off I was just hanging on for the ride. I had to learn how to run things very quickly, as the growth rate demanded new expertise all the time and I was the only one doing all of the work. The fourth year went just as quickly. By 1999, over 1000 stores across Australia were stocking the Attitude brand. I ran the entire warehousing operation from my parents' garage and then my home garage until the end of 1999.

The brand started off with slogan-based t-shirts, slogans which just like me are sarcastic with a positive influence, such as:

I DON'T CARE HOW GOOD YOU ARE
... I'M BETTER

WINNERS MAKE IT HAPPEN ...
LOSERS LET IT HAPPEN

LET'S WORK AS A TEAM AND DO IT MY
WAY!

I DON'T HAVE AN ATTITUDE PROBLEM ...
YOU HAVE A PERCEPTION PROBLEM

IT'S ALL ABOUT LUCK ...
JUST ASK ANY LOSER

© Attitude Inc.®

The national media picked up the story of Attitude Gear®. The fact that I had started with only $50 seemed to be a big factor. I never saw that point as something to boast about; I thought a 25-year-old having only $50 was a bit embarrassing. Nevertheless, I saw this media exposure as a ray of sunshine. Instead of having to pay thousands of dollars to advertise in magazines, I could use the media coverage to grow the brand. After this I must say that I found starting and running a business easy. It was all an attitude (if you excuse the pun).

In 1999, I entered a period that would shape the future of my company and set me closer to reaching my goals and dreams. One day in 1999 I was sitting in my office at home, processing orders, when the marketing manager of Philips Electronics Australia Ltd rang to ask if I would come into their office the next day to discuss a business concept.

I quickly dismissed the invitation, thinking one of my mates was having a lend of me, but she convinced me she was serious. We met the next day, and the company discussed their willingness to license the Attitude logo from me to place on a range of 'Philips with Attitude' stereos. I agreed to the deal.

Thanks to the media exposure I had received over the years, Attitude Gear® was an easily recognised brand. Now I had a major international company wanting to align with my brand. The Philips with Attitude® products went through the roof. Then I started getting more calls to license the brand, from snack food companies to mobile phone manufacturers to local car dealerships. Everyone seemed to be wanting a bit of Attitude.

In 2001 I licensed the whole brand. There are over 60 products now, which include:

Attitude menswear®
Attitude women's wear®
KWA® (kids with attitude) for 2–7 years
Attitude junior® for 7–14 years
Attitude BMX bikes®
Attitude helmets®
Attitude skateboards®
Attitude basketballs®
Attitude basketball backboards®
Attitude backpacks and sports bags®
Attitude boxer shorts®

Attitude body boards®
Attitude shoes®
Attitude hats®
Attitude in-line and roller skates® and associated products
And there are many more products on the way.

To be totally honest, I never thought that I would end up where I am seven years after starting. Sure I had great plans and dreams that I was hoping would work, but the reality is that I didn't have a clue what I was doing in the beginning. All I knew was that I wanted to succeed at something. My attitude was the only factor that got me to this point.

Face the hurdles

In those first years there were days where on the outside I was feeling total despair about the hurdles I had to jump, but deep inside I was still determined to succeed. It was that driving force of wanting to succeed that I believe helped me to be where I am today.

What hurdles are you facing in your life? To jump them you have to do one simple thing. You need to face them. There is no point turning away from them and heading in the other direction. Sooner or later you will just face another hurdle, but this time you will be further away from your goals and dreams. It is your attitude and your attitude alone that will either get you through the problems and challenges in your life, or lead you to run from those problems and challenges.

You can overcome anything in life before it even happens to you. To do this you need to have an attitude that says 'I am going to succeed; I am not going to let my circumstances rule where I will end up in life'. If you want a better job, be a better employee. If you want good or loyal friends, be a better friend. It is that easy.

When my business took off, I did not have the qualifications to run it, but I did not let that minor detail affect my thinking. I know that I could have done some things better. It was all a process. Changing your attitude today does not mean that when you wake up tomorrow everything will be perfect. It requires work, and a lot of it.

Failure is not the end

The question I have most frequently been asked over the last seven years is, 'What would have happened if you had failed?' The answer is easy. I would have tried and succeeded at something else. I have never viewed failure as the end. Failure should never be a full stop in anyone's life.

I have a somewhat distorted view of failure. I see failure as succeeding. I know that you are probably scratching your head right now wondering what I am talking about. Let me explain.

My father used to say to us as we were growing up, 'If you aim at the stars and hit a light post, be happy. At least you have hit something.' He was so right. If you try to achieve something and it does not work out the way you planned, do not let what the world calls 'failing' get you down. You have, simply by trying to achieve something, moved on in your life; you are further ahead than when you started.

Not everything we do in life will always work but, by at least giving things a go, we move in a forward direction.

The only way we can fail is if we never learn from our past experiences.

My wife Vanessa is a good case study when it comes to this point. Vanessa has had a few jobs over the years. She never had a problem getting the positions she applied for. Her problem was that once she landed the job, she would start to worry about the tasks involved. She would nearly talk herself out of taking a position purely because she would convince herself she could not complete the tasks involved properly. All she could see were the new things that she had to learn, and what might happen if she didn't do the job properly. In reality, when she started a new job, she took to it like a duck to water. She had to learn new tasks; she had to increase her level of learning; so she did. If Vanessa had let her attitude of not wanting to fail stay in her head, she would probably still be back in the first job she started with.

HOW MANY THINGS DO YOU JUST ACCEPT BECAUSE YOU ARE TOO SCARED OF FAILING?

You need to understand that unless you step out of your comfort zone and try new things and new challenges, your attitude (and that's the controlling factor in your life) will always rule your direction.

Try and adapt what you have read in this chapter into your life and situations. Don't let a bad attitude towards others, or even yourself, get in the way and slow you down. It is such a simple thing to keep an eye on.

the psychology of success | 2 |

2

WINNERS MAKE IT HAPPEN ...
LOSERS LET IT HAPPEN!

There is an old saying that goes 'Success is a journey, not a destination'.

That is so true. Too many people get caught up in the whole façade of success instead of actually seeing what success requires. Success is a process. Being successful is all about what you need to change, what you need to address, not just what you need to accomplish.

I believe that the only time you can truly call yourself 'successful' is when you have achieved the goals and dreams you have set for yourself. You need to determine that you will make success a lifestyle; that way, everything you do will in turn become successful, whether it be in your business, work or personal life.

The journey to being successful can be made easier if you understand what success actually entails. We all want the best things for our lives, but many times we don't actually understand what is required or what is needed to get those things. With success comes the spoils. Just how badly do you want to be successful? And when do you want to start?

I have developed what I call 'the Psychology of Success'. This is a breakdown of each letter in the word 'success' to highlight what is actually needed to push you into the world of success. By understanding these seven keys, you will be able to enjoy various successes in your personal and business life.

There are many people I call 'one-hit wonders'. All they want is to be successful no matter what the cost. They don't look at the long term—what they want is success, and as quickly as possible. All they are looking at is the end result, the big picture. The problem with that is they forget to account for all the work, the effort and the time that it will take to get there. While success in whatever you do is the ultimate goal, I would rather see longer-term sustained success that was more of a lifestyle than a one-off. Unless you address certain areas of your thinking and who you are, the success that you may create will only be short lived.

Let's now look at what I believe are the true factors that being successful entails:

SACRIFICE
UNDERSTANDING
COMMITMENT
CHARACTER
EXCELLENCE
STRUCTURE
SATISFACTION

These seven keys give you an insight into what success is actually all about. Success is not a label but a process; if mastered it will take you well on your way to fulfilling those goals and dreams of yours.

Sacrifice

This is a word that many of us don't like to hear. If you want to reach your goals and dreams, then you will have to sacrifice things along the way. Whether it is time, friends or finances, you will definitely need to sacrifice something, if not many things. Being successful doesn't just happen. The things you may need to give up, which when you think about them may be too much to bear, will be worth it in the end only if you choose to follow it through to the end result.

I was training at my friend's gym and swimming centre one morning. As I arrived at 6.30 am I noticed many children, only 10–14 years old, doing lap after lap in the pool. I never train at this time normally so I asked one of the instructors what was happening. He told me that this was the young swimming squad that trained every morning and afternoon, six days a week, 50 weeks a year. I asked what they were training for; the Olympics, he replied.

Aren't they a bit young for the next Olympics? I asked. The answer for most of them was yes. So why train now if their best shot isn't for at least 6–8 years? Sacrifice, was the answer.

You see, these kids understood one of the keys to reaching their own success. They needed to sacrifice their mornings and afternoons if they were going to reach their goals and dreams. Very rarely will you become an overnight success.

Even if you do, it is quite probable that success will fade away just as quickly.

It is the lessons we learn when we sacrifice what is dear to us so that we can reach our goals that will inevitably be the key to our successes. What are you willing to give up to achieve your goals and dreams? If you have no answer to this question, then you have to look hard at whether you really want to reach those goals.

At such an early age, those children training at the pool every day understood this key principle. I am sure they would prefer some mornings to sleep in, especially in the middle of winter. But if they are going to have at least a shot at reaching their ultimate goal, the Olympics, then the sacrifices they make today will be the rewards they may reap in their tomorrows.

Do you need to be better qualified to get better pay? If the answer to that question is yes, then get off your backside and enrol in a course. Don't wait for your employer to offer to pay for the course or suggest that you start one. Take the initiative and start today. Yes, that will probably mean less free time with your friends and family, and more study, but yes, it will also bring you closer to your goals and dreams. Do you need to spend late nights organising your business? Then do it. It may not be enjoyable but just think of the end result.

Dean, my brother, is sometimes up until 4 or 5 am drawing plans for his clients. The looks on their faces when he presents them with a plan of their dream home, with the dream land-scape surrounds, is worth all that effort and extra time. It may not be that enjoyable to be working at 4 am in the morning, but in doing this he is sacrificing his own time for his dream.

The sacrifices you make today will make success taste just that little bit sweeter in the end.

Understanding

One of the most important questions you need to ask yourself is, 'Why do I do what I do?' I have met many people in the past few years who are following a path in their lives when they are unsure of where it will lead them or how long it will take to get there. To reach your goals and become successful at everything you put your hand and mind to, you need to understand both what it will take and where you are going. Understanding what is needed to reach those goals and to achieve those dreams is one of the most important, if not the most important, keys to grasp.

When I first started Attitude Inc.® I had absolutely no idea what was involved in running my own business. I had to make a decision very early on that this was a path in my life that I wanted to head down. To do that I needed to understand where it was going to lead.

Don't jump into the latest get-rich scheme or the biggest paying job just because it seems like a good idea at the time. Once you have established what it is that your goals and dreams are, you need to have an understanding of what it is actually going to take to get you there. If you have employees, understanding this key is very important.

As an employer your level of understanding has to be bigger or greater than that of someone who doesn't have employees. What I mean by that is those employees who are working for you will have issues, goals and dreams of their own. The day that you decide to actually understand those issues, goals and dreams will be the day your employees will start being of value instead of a pain. Let me explain.

As a business owner, your employees are essentially working to help you achieve all that you have set out to achieve. Sure, they get paid each week and their jobs put food on their tables and pay their bills, but ultimately they are helping you achieve what you want out of life. Imagine if you could get them to work harder, smarter and more efficiently. The key to making this happen is to understand that your employees all have their own goals and dreams. What you as the employer have to do is find out what those goals and dreams are. Once you have done that you need to help them achieve them. This has a seesaw effect. It is the old 'you scratch my back and I'll scratch yours' theory. Your employees will stop seeing you as the boss who is only after harder work and more of their time and start seeing you as someone who wants them to succeed in their own lives. The harder you help them achieve what they want out of their lives, the harder they will repay the favour by understanding that you have an interest in their personal future.

You see, as employers we all have to understand what our employees are motivated by. I don't mean money; I mean ambition, drive and the desire to achieve their own goals. There is nothing more rewarding than assisting others towards their goals. And just imagine that while you are helping them achieve all they can, they are working towards you achieving your goals and dreams. This worked fantastically in my own business and I know it is a principle that will turn around your staff's attitudes.

Understanding what you want out of your life and/or business is not that complicated. The key is to understand which direction you need to head in and know how many people will be there with you along the way.

Commitment

How committed are you towards your success, your dreams or your goals?

Do they consume your thinking or do you just hope that one day you will maybe achieve them? Many of us tend to take the easy way out when it comes to completing what we desire.

It is quite easy to measure your commitment to your success. Just ask yourself, if something better came along today, would I take it? If you answered 'yes', then it is quite obvious that what you are trying to achieve, your goals and dreams, is not a burning passion within you. Commitment is you saying to yourself that you are going to stay focused on your goals, your dreams and your success through thick and thin, through the highs and the lows.

STAY FOCUSED AND FORGE AHEAD TOWARDS YOUR ULTIMATE GOALS AND DREAMS

The one factor separating successful people from those who aren't is that the successful ones never gave up. You can read many stories of people who had very large and successful businesses, went broke and then came back in a bigger and better way. Their commitment to their ultimate goal never changed, it just took some battering along the way. The level of commitment needed to fulfil those dreams and goals will be more than you have had to use before.

Let's go back for a minute to those young swimmers who were training twice a day. The probability of every one of them competing in the Olympics is fairly remote. But even the ones that miss out will be further ahead in their lives as a direct result of their commitment.

You see, if you understand each of the seven keys to success, it won't matter if you fall short of your expected outcome because you will be in front next time as a result of understanding and applying them. When you are committed to succeeding and reaching your goals your eyes are firmly focused on the end prize. You have made the decision and you are set on completing that direction until the end.

I was watching television one night with my daughter, and a nature show started. It was all about how lizards function and survive. A piece about the chameleon lizard really fascinated me, and I learnt a very valuable lesson which can be applied to our own lives. The chameleon has the talent of being able to blend in with its surroundings, but even more remarkable is its ability to look in a different direction with each of its two eyes. Once one eye spots a potential food target, the chameleon must bring the other eye to focus on the target. It can only commit itself to attacking its prey when it can see it with both eyes.

As I was watching this, I thought to myself that many of us forget to use this same principle on our journey to success. We tend to focus on the doing instead of on the end result, the bigger picture. We need to focus on where we are heading. We need to be committed that we are going to be successful no matter what comes our way. Stop looking around for something easier.

Character

Your character will be the ultimate test of whether your success is long and fruitful or short lived. I have been amazed at the shallowness of character that I have encountered over my short time in business. I have had people promise me the world and deliver nothing and I have had people lie point-blank to my face just to get themselves ahead.

When I first decided to license the entire business, I was very green in that part of the operation, so I thought it best to enlist the services of one of the numerous licensing companies operating internationally. Now I really know the ins and outs of who buys my products and why, so I was bringing a lot of valuable information to the party.

After a few months, I started to realise that the licensing company I had chosen might not be as good as they had made out. The license agreements that had been made were all the direct results of my own efforts in finalising them. When one of my major retailers expressed concern about the licensing company's dealings, and its understanding of my brand, I decided it was time to part company. You should have seen the paperwork that came across my desk, the insults, the abuse and the legal threats. Just a few days earlier they were taking me out to lunch, telling me how good it was to have my brand on board, and now here they were calling me every name under the sun. The president of the company rang and personally abused me.

The one thing I learnt that day is that character will come out in the end. I could have fought their fight. I could have become nasty just like them. But I was determined to rise above their level and not conduct myself in the same manner. The character that you portray will attract the same type of character in those around you.

If you want success in your life, then you will have to make sure you are of the highest character. Your character will be tested every day with issues that come across your desk or into your workplace. Your character is the factor that distinguishes you from the next person.

You will find that successful people are one of a kind. Sure, you can model yourself after a successful person, but ultimately you cannot copy their character or their ethics. They have to be yours and they have to be real.

I have been observing lately, in the newspapers and on the television news, the number of high-fliers who have come unstuck. These business people were the toast of the business world just months ago, and now they are in disgrace. While you could have looked at them and said to yourself that they were the ultimate picture of success, the truth is that a lot of areas were lacking. I believe the biggest of these was character. Having the outward signs of success is not nearly enough. It is all too fake and easily lost. True success starts from within us all. You need to make sure that your character is of the highest standard; that your ethics both in business and in your personal life are as they should be.

A truly successful person will have many people following them. But with that comes responsibility. You are responsible for those who now watch you, whether it is your employees, your employer or even your friends and family.

Good character isn't dealt out to those who are in high-paying or important positions; it is a gift and, if recognised, can be a great tool in reaching your dreams and goals.

Your character will show when the times are tough. Do you give up or do you keep going? Do you let other people tell you what you want out of life, or do you stay focused and commit yourself to reaching what you want out of life?

Excellence

Whatever you do, do it well. That is one bit of advice my father gave all us kids as we were growing up. We never had any pressure from our parents as to what career path we should pursue. The only thing I remember my father saying on the subject of careers is: 'If you are going to be a garbageman that is fine with us, as long as you are the best garbageman that you can be.' Success will require excellence. Long-term success will require excellence to be a part of who you are. There is no use excelling at just one area of your life. You need to make every part of your life count—excellence in attitude, habits, marriage, family life, work, in everything.

NEVER SETTLE FOR SECOND BEST WHEN
IT COMES TO STRIVING FOR SUCCESS
OR REACHING YOUR GOALS

If you are focused on excelling at everything you put your hand to, your journey will be more enjoyable and permanent.

If you are successful you have already stood out from the crowd, you have achieved more than others—this is one of the meanings for success. Whether you keep that success will be reliant on the level of effort and excellence you attach to everything you do from that point on.

I have already talked about my brother Dean and his land-scaping business. He is a good example to illustrate this point of excellence. As Dean landscapes million-dollar-plus homes there is a level of excellence he has had to present as a standard service. The owners of these homes are in the top income bracket and most are dealing with excellence as a daily occurrence.

I remember Dean telling me of a time when he was meeting with a client and the architect to pitch for the business. The client was about to spend over $3 million on the house and around $1.5–2 million on the landscaping.

This was a major client, and Dean had worked night and day to prepare for this meeting. He had drawn up the plans in scale form, he had colour-enhanced them and had the most precise details attached. The value of those plans would have been around $6000. He was totally prepared for the meeting. He had set a level of excellence that the client was used to.

The architect was to show his plans first. He got up, unrolled a sheet of paper and said here it is. The client was less than impressed. There was no detail, let alone a feeling of sat-isfaction that the money he had paid for the plans was money well spent. Then it was Dean's turn. By the time he had rolled out his drawing he could see the look of satisfaction on the client's face. That architect didn't get the job, but Dean did.

You see, it is the extra mile you take that will be the one

that leads you closer to your dreams and goals. Successful people don't just do what is required; they excel themselves and do what's not expected.

I also have an older sister. Everything that Sharlene does, she does with a level of excellence. When she was at university she aimed at distinctions and high distinctions. She became not just a teacher but an excellent teacher. Now she is married and has two children. Sharlene has carried the same level of excellence that she set as her educational and employment benchmark into her personal and family life.

Structure

Success requires structure. To reach your goals and your dreams you need to know what is involved. You need to structure yourself and your direction. Please don't forget about your personal life either. There needs to be balance and structure in both your business and your personal life. If there is no structure in your personal life, you may tend to become a bit of a workaholic, which in the end may lead to more problems than benefits.

Like a fine-tuned car that runs on premium fuel, the best of engine oils and the proper parts, so your whole life should be structured and balanced in the same fashion. You need the best ingredients in your pursuit of your goals and dreams.

The importance of balance between your personal and business or work life cannot be over-emphasised. With success or the striving to become successful comes a tendency to get caught up in the whole process. Unless you are very careful, it is all too easy to burn yourself out and actually move further away from your goals.

Your social life is an integral part of the whole success process. It is the time away from your work or your business that has the potential to recharge your batteries. Burning yourself out is of no use to you or those around you. You need to structure yourself and your time in a way that will take you closer to the goals you have set for yourself.

Never just plan to achieve your goals; you need to plan to enjoy yourself along the way. What is the point of doing everything for your family, making money for that nice house, sending your children to that great school or buying that nice car, if you never get to see them? The family and friends around you need to stay just that: around you!

Don't push everyone away, thinking that once you 'make it' you can just pick up where you left off. You need to take them along for the ride. I love telling my friends and family where I am at in relation to my goals. I have friends who share their stories as well. It not only brings you closer to each other and part of each other's dreams, it also makes you accountable in a way.

Imagine building a house; while it might look great when it's finished, it doesn't start that way. There needs to be a lot of work and effort put into place. First the foundation needs to be set. Without a firm and solid foundation the house will probably fall over. The same principle applies in your journey to success.

The foundation you set for yourself has to be strong enough to hold your dreams and goals. By that I mean, if you put little time and care into the preparation of what is needed, then in all likelihood your dream will fall over and amount to nothing.

Make sure you have the structure and the balance you need in the pursuit of your goals and dreams. Being successful will require a lot of time, effort and planning—so get it right the first time.

Satisfaction

There is an important rule to becoming successful. Be satisfied. This doesn't necessarily mean that you are content, just that you are happy with where you are at.

I had a man in my office recently who wanted my opinion on where he should venture next in his employment. Why he thought I would know I wasn't too sure, so I asked him to tell me about his past jobs. He started by saying that he had had many jobs but unfortunately his employers didn't appreciate his way of working. I probed a little bit further. Every time he moved jobs it seemed to be a step up, but the problem was that he was not satisfied with the new job even before he took it. He did well at his jobs but 'none of them gave him the satisfaction he was desiring'.

I believe he missed this very important key, the key of satisfaction. A job will never keep him satisfied. It is 'himself' that needs to make him satisfied wherever he is.

Wherever you are in your life or employment as you read this book, remember to take satisfaction in where you are. Be satisfied with how you got there.

You may be way off where you wanted to be, but until you come to terms with the now, you will never be able to handle the future.

I wanted a worldwide brand when I first started my business. I wanted everything in the first week. I wanted it all! It wasn't until I became satisfied with the small things that I was able to focus on the bigger issues.

It is very easy to say, 'If only I was rich, I would be satisfied.' The odds are that you wouldn't be. You need to be happy with what you have now to be happy with what you may get later on. Be happy with what you have achieved. There will be many who will come across your path who will let you know all the negatives, so don't join their party.

Negative people come and go but true satisfaction will stay forever. Being successful isn't easy. If it were, then everyone would be successful.

So if you do get to live your dream or reach your goals, then why would you not be satisfied? Along the way you can take great satisfaction in the knowledge that you are at least trying to better yourself, you are trying to better those around you, your friends, family and maybe even employees. If that isn't enough to give you satisfaction then I don't know what would.

As you can see, there is a lot more to success than just a label. True success is long term. While you can be successful at small things along the way, I am really talking about reaching your goals and dreams.

At this point I suggest you go find a piece of paper. Write down the seven keys I've just described, and see if you have mastered any of them. Remember though, true success is a journey—it isn't a tag you can apply to just a few things you have achieved. I guarantee that if you follow those keys, or apply them to what you are doing now in your life, not only will it make your path a bit clearer, it will also make the journey just a little bit more enjoyable.

never stop learning |3|

3

THINK YOU CAN,
THINK YOU CAN'T,
EITHER WAY
YOU ARE RIGHT!

© Attitude Inc.®

It amazes me even today, the number of 'experts' out there. You know the type, the ones who 'know it all'. I have never subscribed to the theory that I know it all, although if you talk to my wife she may tell you that I think I do. Knowledge, true knowledge, I believe, comes from experience and learning. By that, I mean that as we go through life, we need to grow, not only physically but also mentally.

One of the problems we face as we grow older is that we tend to hang onto what we know is tried and trusted in our own lives. The only way to grow, whether in business or your personal life, is to step out and 'give it a go'. The longer you put off advancing towards those goals and dreams, the longer it will take you to make them a reality.

As someone who didn't really excel at schooling, I have always wondered what would have happened if I applied myself just a little bit harder, pushed myself just that little bit further.

I am a big fan of learning from life's experiences; unfortunately, many of us don't let life teach us anything, or we quickly dismiss 'bad' experiences. We know that if we can control certain areas of our lives, we have a safety net. While it is great to be living safely and not taking too many risks, not 'giving things a go' is going to slow you down on your journey towards achieving your goals. You will end up accepting the same outcomes and most probably staying the same distance away from your goals. We need to prepare ourselves for our future so that with that future comes change.

Life will inevitably throw us all a curve ball at some stage. In 1987, at the age of 17, I was involved in a major motorcycle accident. I was at a wedding and a new acquaintance offered me a lift to the reception on the back of his motorcycle. Being like any 17-year-old, I accepted with great haste. The only catch was that we had to stop on the way to pick up our helmets. I know what you are thinking, but I was only 17 and full of adventure.

On the way to pick up the helmets we were struck by a car doing a U-turn. We were stupidly doing in excess of 100 kilo-metres an hour and the impact threw me through the car's windscreen and underneath a parked car.

To say that we put a dampener on the wedding is an under-statement. There was only one route from the church to the reception place and that was past the accident site. I had sustained major injuries, fracturing my femur in numerous places and, due to not having a helmet, I had major head and facial injuries.

A few days later, when I eventually came to in the hospital, I was a mess. I could not remember anything that had happened. All I knew was that I didn't look like me, my leg was swollen from the operation and I had tubes sticking out of every part of my body. And I mean every part. I was in that hospital as a direct result of a bad decision.

Over the next six months, I had to learn how to perform the simplest tasks. I had to learn how to walk again. Talk about taking things for granted! You know the saying 'you don't know what you've got until you lose it'? It was so true. There were months and months of painful recovery sessions.

Now I never asked or planned for this to happen. It wasn't part of my ultimate scheme to get ahead in life, but I had to meet that hurdle face-on. However, as a 17-year-old facing a huge amount of time lying in a bed, my mind was not firmly planted in thinking about the future.

I was blaming everyone for the situation I was in. Except myself. But, I was the one who decided to get on that motorbike. I was the one who decided not to have a helmet on, and I was the one who was keen to go as fast as we could.

Now that being the case, I was the one that had to take charge of my life. I had to learn from this experience. No one else but me had to take responsibility for the actions that led me to this dilemma. I have to say it took me a long time to come to terms with where my life was at. I didn't just wake up one morning and decide that I was in self-pity mode and it was time to get out.

If I'd known back then what we are about to go through in this chapter, the road to my getting out of my self-pity state would have been a lot quicker. Over a long period, I slowly realised that I had an awesome opportunity. I could start all over again or I could let my circumstances take control over my life and force me into being someone and something that I was not.

We all know people who have had stuff happen to them, whether in their businesses or their personal lives, that does not seem fair. While it would be fair to say that those people have every right to feel sorry for themselves, it actually does no good for them in the end. If we don't learn from the good and bad experiences that life throws us, we will continue to go around that same roundabout not being able to see the exit.

I am a big advocate of the theory that everything happens for a reason. I might not like what happens sometimes but I am forced to handle those issues head on, to learn from those experiences and grow from them. Good and bad experiences will inevitably come your way throughout your life. It is what action you take at that exact time that will either force you closer or further away from achieving your goals.

I believe that there are three levels of learning, which I call zones—the comfort zone, the learning zone and the wild zone.

The comfort zone

Human beings love being comfortable. We don't like being put in a position where we are not in control for too long.

This however, while it may be 'secure', is not that healthy. All of us are guilty of too often staying well within the boundaries of the comfort zone. How many times have you decided not to join in something because it was out of your comfort zone?

Whether in life or in business, you will eventually be faced with a situation or challenge that you will need to venture out of your comfort zone to complete. Now I know what you are thinking: 'I only do things that I am comfortable with or comfortable in completing.' How boring! The whole purpose for being on this planet is to excel. The only way to excel is to be trying new things and making ourselves better every day.

Imagine eating the same food for every meal every day, every week, every year for the rest of your life; let's say meat and potatoes. While you would probably still live a long life, the essence of that life, without enjoying new taste sensations, would be quite dull. The same principle applies to our lives. If you only do the same-old same-old every day, not trying new experiences, not allowing yourself to step out and be challenged, then sure, you may still live a life of some satisfaction, but wouldn't it be great to get to the end of your life not regretting anything, not wishing 'if only'.

When I was first asked to speak publicly a few years ago, I came up with every excuse under the sun why I couldn't do it. Mind you, I have always had the desire to impact people's lives, so you would think that speaking to different crowds, some with hundreds of delegates, would achieve that in a faster fashion. Nevertheless I was in fear; this was way out of my comfort zone. How many times have you had opportunities that have gone begging purely as a result of not stepping out and grabbing what should have been yours?

In 1995 I was managing a gym in the western suburbs of Sydney. I was totally within my comfort zone. I could do that job with my eyes tied behind my back—but after a while it became mundane and boring. Now this was the same job that I had been doing for a while, so what changed? I did. My level of learning had stopped. I had reached a point where I knew what was expected, what was required, and I only met those expectations. Was this the fault of the business owner? Well, yes and no. Yes, because to increase your staff's potential you must always be aware if and when they start to outgrow the challenges put before them. No, because I was not being challenged within my job, and consequently I was taking the easy way out. I was the one who had decided that I was not going to learn anything more at that job. I had made the subconscious decision that I would just cruise along.

Let me give you another example. The other day I spent some time in the garden with my wife Vanessa and our daughter Jade, getting rid of weeds. Jade asked if she could do the front garden while we did the backyard. After about 20 minutes, she came to inform us that she had finished. We were a bit concerned by this, as it had taken us the same amount of time to do just a small section of the back garden. The thought that we were getting slow and old crossed our minds very quickly. I decided to go and have a look at the job Jade had done. Sure, there were no weeds to be seen. But she had only weeded what could be seen from the pathway. When we looked through the garden, there were weeds everywhere.

Jade's comment was, 'No one sees those.' She was right, you had to really get in there and seek them out, but it was the ones that no one saw that were causing the main problems.

How many times do you work only to the minimum requirement, or complete a task that just scrapes through? True, that is all that is expected sometimes, but there is no learning, or breaking out of our comfort zones, if all we ever do is what we are comfortable with. Just remember that it is the unconfronted issues that 'no one' sees that eventually will keep us in our comfort zone, leaving us the same old boring persons with the same old boring problems for the rest of our lives. You really need to have a good hard look at your life, your actions, and maybe even your personality for any deep-seated issues that may be causing you to always fall short of your dreams.

Comfort zones are just that, comfortable, but try and step out once in a while and see what will happen.

The learning zone

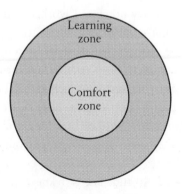

The learning zone is the most important one. To grow we need to learn. Spending time (most of our lives) within our comfort zones is perfectly all right, perfectly safe, but it's average. There is nothing wrong with doing that; it just won't allow you to grow into the person you need to be to achieve those goals you have set for yourself. To grow and move closer to achieving those goals, we need to spend time in the learning zone.

The longer you spend in the learning zone the bigger your comfort zone will get; and the bigger your comfort zone gets, the easier it is to fulfil your dreams and desires. The learning zone becomes less of an effort. It becomes second nature.

After my motorcycle accident I was faced with a new level of learning. I had to learn how to walk all over again. This may seem an easy process to the uninitiated—after all, it's something we do every day—but I was finding it quite difficult. Imagine if I had decided one day to give up, that I didn't want the pain and the frustration, that I didn't want to learn how to walk again. I would still be sitting in that bed. I had to make a decision early on that my level of learning was going to have to go up a few notches. I worked and worked at that walking. I was not comfortable with sitting in a wheelchair, hoping that one day my leg would just repair itself. I was determined to complete every task set out for me to do.

How often are you that way inclined? When obstacles or challenges are put in front of you, do you decide to see them through no matter how hard or how long it takes? Or do you decide to take the fastest and easiest way out, not fully completing the task?

When I started Attitude Inc.® I knew absolutely nothing

about business. All I knew was that I wanted to succeed. I had to learn the different techniques that go with owning and running a business. While my methods may not have been conventional, I was still able (quite successfully) to master the finer arts of business managing and ownership.

One thing I decided very early on was to surround myself with people who were smarter than I was. If I was to grow my business I needed people around me who knew more about business than I did. (That wasn't really too hard!) I set out to meet people I saw as successes in their own industries. I wanted to know what made them tick, what drove them, and what they did or didn't like about my business model.

The one place I didn't go was to people in the clothing industry. Their views would be tainted and directed by their past experiences within that industry. I talked to people who would give me their advice from a purely business perspective, with no past experiences colouring their attitude. I had to be a blank sheet of paper, ready for someone to draw on. I was determined that I was going to suck as much information out of these people as I could. I must say that not everyone accommodated my request to talk. I think some of them thought I was after them to invest money in my business, but I wasn't. I wanted to be smarter, I wanted to learn by asking the right people the right questions.

Recently we moved into a new home. In the backyard was a beautiful fishpond, a water feature. Our daughter asked if we could put some goldfish in it, so we went to the local aquarium to see what was there. Being like most 10-year-olds, Jade decided she wanted the biggest fish, the koi carp. As the fishpond is not overly large, it turned out that these fish would be a bit big. After talking to the salesperson about what my daughter wanted and what we could actually put into the pond, it occurred to me that these fish could teach us all a lot about our lives.

Koi carp start out around the same size as your average goldfish. The difference is that they grow to suit their environment. If you have a huge pond, they could grow to about 40–60 centimetres. If you have a somewhat smaller pond, they would only grow to suit their surroundings (but they were still too big for our pond).

This illustrates the principle that we need to encourage in our own lives, but unfortunately, we tend to take the easy way out. You will only grow when you step out of your comfort zone. The bigger the comfort zone you create for yourself by doing this, the more opportunities will come your way, the more success and the more goals you will accomplish.

Swim in a bigger pond. As you learn more about life and all that living entails, ensure that you grow from those experiences. We all need to learn from every mistake and every experience that we go through. That way, as we get older we get wiser, and as we get wiser, the quality of our lives is enhanced by the surroundings we have created.

When life hands you a problem or when dramas come your way, you have two choices:

1. Just let it affect the rest of your life and those around you, or
2. Learn to grow to meet the demands of that problem.

I am not one to handle dramas particularly easily, or at least I wasn't when I first started my business. I had to learn not to let problems that were out of my control affect my dreams and desires. These days, when a problem comes my way I have it solved within record time, as I am not going to let it affect my lifestyle.

Once I recognised that problems were inevitably going to turn up from time to time, I was able to meet and conquer them. We need not to panic, but to sit back and evaluate the reality of the situation. Chances are that the problem is not as big as we first thought and can be handled quite easily.

Like the koi carp, we too can grow into our surrounds—but most of us don't realise that. Why be a little fish in a big pond when you can grow bigger? Why let your surrounds affect your future and destiny? Next time something that is certain to stretch you comes across your path, just remember the koi carp and adapt to the situation.

The wild zone

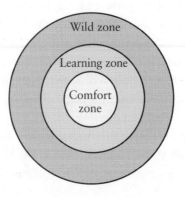

I have also spent quite a lot of time in the wild zone. This is a place you don't want to be in too often, and when you are there you want to get out of it ASAP. You know, it's when you have started a business venture and then figured out you are in way over your head, or your personal life is going every which way but up and it is all becoming too hard.

We will all end up in the wild zone at some point of our lives. How long we stay there is totally up to us. You will know when you are in your wild zone—it feels the total opposite of being in your comfort zone.

While that may sound obvious, you would be amazed at the number of people who over the years have asked my advice about businesses that are in turmoil. When I sit down with them, it is so easy to see that they have so lost control of their situation that they can't see the right way out. The wild zone could also be defined as doing things without thinking, or jumping into a situation only to think after the fact.

I love the word 'hindsight'. You know, you always hear it when someone has stuffed up and they are trying to justify their actions. 'Well, in hindsight I should have got that contract checked by my solicitor' or 'in hindsight I should have had a pest inspection'. You know quite well, and I have been there myself, that sometimes when you are in the middle of something you will have a little feeling that something doesn't feel quite right. If you don't act on that feeling, it may all go pear-shaped and blow up and out.

If we spent a bit more time crossing the t's and dotting the i's, we wouldn't spend so much time in the wild zone, which normally leads to problems. When you come to realise that every decision you make will affect whether you reach your goals and dreams, you will start to make your decisions a lot more cautiously.

You really don't want to put yourself through the torment and frustration of the wild zone time after time. When you are in the wild zone you will know it. You have no control of your situation, and everything seems to go from bad to worse, your time and effort is wasted. Get out of there straight away and remember what it was like.

Putting it together
Now that you can see these three distinct zones you need to put them together in a way that works for you.

You need to live within your comfort zone, but if you want to excel in life you need to change and grow. The only way to do that is to be constantly spending time within the learning zone. That doesn't necessarily mean you need to go and enrol at university and become a scholar; what it means is that you need to experience new thought processes, new ways of doing things, get a bigger circle of friends who can challenge you in new and exciting ways.

If you feel you have 'learnt all there is to know' within your life or within your business, you may as well just roll over and die. I do not believe that we will ever know everything. Sure, you can be the best at some things, the most knowledgeable about other things, but when it comes to a better existence we need to be constantly looking at improving ourselves.

As I've already said, I knew nothing about owning and running a business when I started. I had no experience at all of the clothing industry. Now let me tell you that if you were to start a clothing company, or any other kind of business, it would be much wiser to have some sort of clue about it. It will save you a lot of time, effort and frustration. All I knew at the time was that there was a hole in the market, and I liked wearing clothes. That was it. That was not nearly enough. I had a big problem. I had to learn and I had to learn fast— and I mean fast. Attitude Inc.® took off so quickly I barely had time to scratch myself. I had no choice but to learn as I was going. But I did recognise very quickly that if I didn't become a bit smarter, my efforts up to that point would be wasted, purely as a result of being pig-headed.

Knowing nothing about the ins and outs of starting a company could have lost me my business before I had really got started. For example, I didn't know I had to have a trade-mark, didn't know what it was, and certainly didn't know how to get one. If you have ever had to apply for a trademark you will know what I am talking about here: it was and still is an area of great confusion. I had to learn, and learn quickly, what I was up for. I researched the rules until I was quoting them in my sleep. Having chosen the word 'attitude', it would take me over four years and thousands of dollars to actually secure the trademark rights. Did I give up? No. I had to learn this new area of my business.

Whether you choose to go over the hurdles placed in your path, or turn around and give up, is entirely up to you—but I wasn't about to let something stop me before I even got started.

Learning from your mistakes is a big key to advancing, in either life or business. In my first year of business, I was very green. I was brought up in a Christian home; my father is a Christian minister. The values we were raised with I do not regret. When it came to dealing with people, I naively thought that everyone would have the same mentality.

With Attitude Inc.® having taken off the way it did, for a retailer in another state to call me wasn't surprising, and I went to see him a few weeks later as part of my rounds. He placed my biggest order up until then, $36 000, and I was on cloud nine. The brand was getting the recognition and sales it deserved, I thought to myself.

The owner invited me out socially on a few occasions while I was there; he knew everyone and everyone seemed to know him. I was confident that this was the start of a healthy, prosperous business relationship. Back in Sydney, I organised his order and sent it off. Around three weeks later, with no feedback, I decided to see how sales were going and organise payment for the order. He was oddly distant; this wasn't the same person I'd been having a good time with just weeks earlier. I had another trip to his area coming up, so I decided to drop in to the shop he'd opened in a new shopping centre, where I found that not only my products, but all the other stock in the store, was half price or less. I couldn't understand why this would be. Don't forget I was very green at this stage. The owner 'wasn't in', and in a candid chat with one of the floor staff, I discovered she hadn't been paid for over three weeks. She also told me that even before the sale started my products were the fastest selling line they carried. Attempts to contact the owner were in vain. Back in Sydney, I received a call from him to say that things were a bit slow, but he was organising the payment within the next few weeks. Being brought up the way I was, I actually believed him. After the 'few weeks' were up, with no payment in sight, I gave him another call. No answer. The phones were disconnected.

Let me tell you, when you start a business with $50, the last thing you need is to have $36 000 of working capital taken away. I started to worry. I didn't know what I should do. I rang a few of my lawyer friends and explained the situation. The silence at their end of the phone only confirmed that I was in a bit of a pickle. Then it arrived: the letter from his lawyers. He was applying for bankruptcy. Not only that, but since I wasn't a secured creditor, my stock would be sold to pay other people's bills. I was shattered. Here I had trusted what someone had told me and it was all a sham. I found out later that this was not the first of this man's businesses to go under. Many people lost a lot of money from that experience, big companies and small.

What did I learn? Never trust anyone again? Well, no. One bad experience didn't necessarily mean that everyone would treat me the same. Do better homework on people? Absolutely. The only way to stop the same thing happening in the future was to learn from this mistake. It hurt my business for a long time, and I had to fight long and hard to overcome my misfortune, but I wasn't going to let my dream go under because of someone else's mistakes and failings.

To be sure, a degree of bad debt, as any business person will tell you, is a factor that has to be added into the daily equation of owning and running a business, but I made certain I would not be caught out like that again.

It is up to you where you live most of your life, whether it be in your comfort zone, in the learning zone or way out in the wild zone. Just remember, that to grow and to reach those goals and dreams that you have set for yourself, you will have to eventually change something. I challenge you to put this sentence up on your desk, your mirror at home and maybe even in your car.

IF NOTHING CHANGES ... NOTHING CHANGES

If you don't address the change that needs to occur in your life, your circumstances will always stay the same and you will always fall short of reaching your desired outcomes.

setting the standards | 4 |

4

I WOULD RATHER BE DISLIKED
FOR WHAT I AM, THAN BE LIKED
FOR WHAT I AM NOT

© Attitude Inc.®

We all go through life living and operating by a set of standards that we have either set for ourselves or that we became accustomed to as we were growing up. These standards set out the way that we operate, think and even react.

A problem we all face is that if those standards are never looked at or adjusted, we will constantly battle the same issues and problems over and over again. But what do I mean by standards? My definition is in terms of a grade or level of excellence, achievement or advancement, of setting my goals and living by them.

We all find at some time in our lives that we are frustrated when we can't seem to get ahead, whether it be in business, financially or personally. When this happens, the one thing we do not seem to look at is where we have set the bar on what we expect to achieve.

My close friends know that I am black and white when it comes to my outlook on life and how I deal with problems. I really have no sympathy for people who constantly whine and whinge about where they are in life. I am the only person responsible for where I am today, and you are the only person you can blame for where you are today. Sure, there are issues and circumstances that affect where we are today, but it is up to you what you make of them, and only you can steer your life and its direction.

You will undoubtedly already have in mind people you know who are constantly blaming other people for their situations. It may even be you who is making excuses; even now, you may be saying to yourself, 'He doesn't know my situation'. You are totally correct. I do not know your situation, only you do, and as I said before, only *you* can change it.

THE LONGER YOU 'WAIT' FOR OTHER PEOPLE TO 'UNDERSTAND' YOUR SITUATION, THE LONGER YOU DELAY MOVING AHEAD

As most of the world is aware, in 2000 the Olympic Games were held in Sydney. I am not a great fan of track and field sports, but I found myself riveted to the television as the high jump was starting. The qualifying height was 2.28 metres. That was the standard, set for everybody who was willing to give it a go. If you or I had wanted to 'go for gold' in this event, we would have had to qualify months before by reaching a standard just to enter the competition—and then clear 2.28 metres for our first jump.

All of us go through life with an understanding of certain set standards. For example, we have laws to abide by. It is how well we meet those basic standards that dictates how well we will do in our personal lives.

Now, back to the high jump. What would happen if the first competitor who lined up to make his first attempt stopped just before the bar and complained that the height was 'unfair' and he wanted it lower? He would fail.

Some of us go through life trying to set lower standards for ourselves because we think we deserve them to be lower. We move towards our goals and dreams, and just as we are about to jump we give up, because we feel it's going to be too hard. The only way to excel and grow in our lives is to be continually pushing ourselves to be better.

As we were growing up, my father used to come out with positive one-liners. Until I was in my late teens, I had no idea what he was on about. One of them went like this: 'If you aim at nothing, you will always hit it.' That, unfortunately, is how some of us go through this thing we call life. We just 'exist'. What a waste. I do not know about you, but I want to make an impact on everything that I do.

Back to the high jumpers for a minute. When the competitor clears the first height, he is eligible to attempt a second, greater height. As we achieve things and we get better at them, we are able to attempt new challenges. This is due to the fact that the standards we set for ourselves are the template for our success.

Let me give you a personal example. When I decided to start my own business, I had no experience at all. Nearly everyone I mentioned my idea to quickly informed me that statistics showed that 80 per cent of small businesses went under in the first year of operation, and 80 per cent of what was left went under in the second year—and so on. I was determined that I wasn't going to figure in those statistics.

The first goal I set myself was to ignore both the statistics and the people telling me about them. I set my own standards. The first standard I set myself was 'Don't Fail'! Sure, there were some tough times ahead, but since one of my goals was not to fail, my outlook was a bit clearer. I was not focused on the doom and gloom because I was focused on my success.

Not long ago I was asked to be a guest reporter on a television programme. One of my stories was on defensive driving courses for professional drivers. During filming, the instructor highlighted one of the mistakes we all make: we focus our eyes too close to the front of the car, not further ahead where they are supposed to be. For example, when we see a pothole coming up we tend to focus on it; in our heads we say to ourselves, 'I am going to miss that pothole, I am going to miss that pothole'. And what do we do? We hit it. Because we focus on it so strongly the brain directs our actions towards it.

Unfortunately, the same principle applies in our personal and business lives. We focus so much on the small problems and issues (potholes) that we tend to be drawn towards them, then we get stuck in them so that they cause minor, sometimes even major, damage. We should keep our eyes firmly focused on the bigger goals we have set for ourselves. Sure, we will notice the small potholes/issues that arise, but we will not get distracted by them and waste our time on minor issues.

One of my biggest problems in my first year of business was that I was green. Not having any experience, I was really just handling each situation as it came along, the same way I was running my life at that time.

Hold onto your standards

In its first year, the success of Attitude Inc.® attracted a lot of media attention, largely because I had started with only $50. The one thing I must say about success is that it seems to attract all sorts of people to you.

On the other end of the phone one day were two 'business-men' who had to see me straight away because they had something that I needed to see and hear. I am not easily led, but they went into a bit of detail about how they wanted to help me with the brand and how their contacts would help me, so I arranged to meet up with them. When I got there, their 'office' was a garage. That didn't bother me—after all, my business was run out of my garage for the first four years; what did bother me was that they had made themselves out to be a big multinational corporation.

So right from the outset, I was a bit cautious, to say the least. That day was filled with sales pitches to end all sales pitches. They took me to see different retail outlets, different manu-facturers and even potential investors. I wasn't looking for investors at all, but they had decided that they were going to take over my business and its direction. Discussing my plans over lunch, one of them stopped me in mid-sentence and said he thought it would be best to move away from t-shirts and get into business suits. Can you imagine it, Attitude business suits?

I was dumbfounded. Who gave these so-called experts the right to assume that they could control or try to own my dream? By the end of the day, they had told me everything that was wrong with my business, products and future.

Then they introduced me to a woman from New Zealand who owned 12 clothing stores. I decided to forget the earlier part of the day and concentrate on getting my products into her stores. She seemed to like them, and said she would consider stocking the label in all her outlets.

A few weeks passed and I received an order from the two men I had spent the day with for the New Zealand outlets. I had done a bit of checking in the meantime and found the cost of shipping the products over there was so expensive that it would blow the overall cost way out.

Remember that this was early in my business life, and profit margin was all-important. I rang them to let them know that I was going to pass on filling the order. Did I get it! They told me how stupid I was, how unprofessional, how single-minded, even how I was losing sight of the bigger picture.

I was shocked. Here I had made a commonsense decision, and here was someone telling me I was an idiot.

A few weeks later, the New Zealand trademarks office rang to tell me that someone had just registered my trademark in their country. New Zealand television had picked up some of the current affairs and business shows in which I had been highlighted, and someone in the registration office had recognised the logo and done a bit of research. The applicants were the two men who had tried to make me change the direction of my business a few weeks earlier. It took me a few months and a lot of time and money to put a stop to their actions.

The lesson I learnt that week was that other people's standards were not always the same as mine. I would never consider ripping someone off, and I never expected that anyone would do it to me.

You will inevitably come across people whose standards are nowhere near yours. What do you do? Do you lower your standards to match theirs? Or do you rise above them no matter the personal cost, and press on? I must admit the inner me really wanted to belt those guys, but then I would have been operating at their level. I had to regroup quickly and get myself out of a hole that someone else had kindly dug for me.

The true tests of your standards will not come when times are going well. You will always be tested when you are at your lowest. Most of the time the easy way out is just that, easy. You won't end up in a better position, however; you will just be giving up.

I seriously thought I would have to find another career after this incident—but that only lasted about 30 minutes. If I had let my thinking be directed at this 'pothole', I would have been totally consumed by it. Instead, I was determined from that day on that I was not going to let other people's actions dictate where my dream would end.

I have met many other people operating in that same manner, but I can honestly say that I have never let their low standards affect mine, or the direction I wanted to head in. It wasn't always easy, but in the end I was the one who came out on top simply because I refused to be pulled to their level.

The standards that you set in your life will help you achieve what you want. As soon as you lower those standards, you lower the expected outcomes.

Spring-cleaning

Every year I become embroiled in a ritual that seems to haunt every marriage, the dreaded spring-clean. (Most males will understand the pain and torture I am referring to.) From the name of the procedure, you might think that it would happen once a year, but my wife tends to do it a lot more often than that. It always amazes me that most of the items being thrown away at this time seem to be mine. So I do what most husbands do—once the pile is stacked up, I sneak out and take back the things I want to hang on to.

I have used the spring-cleaning principle in my own life. I have had a lot of positive feedback, input and direction over the years, but I have also had a lot of people impart negative feelings, ideas and comments about what I am doing. I am sure you have people like this around you as well. You know, the 'friends' who, when you come up with a great suggestion or idea are the first to let you know that it can't be done or, when you do something that doesn't quite work out the way you planned, are the first to say 'I told you it wouldn't work'.

After a few years of this I reached a point where I really wanted around me the people who were going to push me to reach my goals and dreams, who were helping me set my standards. It is easy being negative; anyone can do it. It was the people who, regardless of the circumstances, could see the bigger picture that I wanted around me.

I was also getting frustrated by people who weren't happy with what they had. They had no ambition to better their circumstances and I was unable to change their thinking. In reality, they were getting no value from their association with me either. There was nothing more frustrating for me than not being able to challenge their thinking in any way.

So spring-cleaning works both ways. On a regular basis I look at who is having an impact on my life. If it is a negative impact, whether in my business life or personal life, I choose to move away from that influence. I do not do it in a 'holier than thou' type of way; that is not what I am trying to achieve. If someone is not improving my thinking and pushing me to achieve more, and if I am not improving their thinking and pushing them to achieve more, I 'spring-clean' them. This may sound harsh, but I can honestly say that this simple process has helped me stay totally focused on what I am trying to achieve and who I really should be.

I challenge you now to write down a list of the people you are in constant contact with, then write next to each name the good influences that person has on your life and goals, and the bad influences. If the negative list is bigger than the positive list, you have to ask yourself whether their influence is keeping you from achieving all you can.

I have had the opportunity over the last few months to train with an ex-professional boxer. He was telling me that when he was training and preparing for a fight, he would choose as his sparring partner another professional boxer in a weight division above his own. The reason was that if he didn't he would be under-training; he would be setting his standard too low. He had to push himself to be better than the person he was about to fight.

So why do we allow ourselves to be influenced by people who are trying to achieve less than we are?

When I first started Attitude Inc.®, I was determined to learn from the best. I set out to meet some of the greatest business identities in this country and a couple that were business legends from overseas. The biggest problem I faced when I approached many of these people was that they thought that I wanted their money.

Once they understood that I just wanted 30 minutes of their time to discuss how they got to where they are, they were a lot more accommodating. I wanted their opinions on what I was trying to achieve, and I wanted to know what hurdles they had faced.

Now I was nowhere near their league in business, but I knew that if I was to make my way there, I needed to know how it was done and what I had to prepare myself to face. I made sure that my standards were set high right from the start. I was under no illusion that I was going to be success-ful overnight, but I also knew that if I set my standards and goals within easy reach I would achieve them early on, and potentially stagnate.

THE IMPOSSIBLE IS WHAT NOBODY CAN DO UNTIL SOMEONE DOES IT

Many of us become stagnant in our personal and business lives, accustomed to the safety of standards that we set years ago.

If you feel that your life has become safe and even stagnant, you need to look seriously at setting new goals and new
standards.

Stop moving the goal posts!

A big Newcastle Knights fan, I love watching a rugby league
match. I find myself riveted to the television sometimes by the
level of commitment and determination to winning that some
teams display. Imagine if a football team decided in the middle
of the game that because they could not break the opposition's
defence, they would like the try line moved closer to them.
Or because the wind picked up just as the kicker was about
to convert a try, he asked the referee to move the goal posts
closer or in the direction of the wind. It just would not happen.
The rules have been set and are known to the teams *before* the
game starts.

Then why is it that when things become hard, some of us
decide to move our personal goal posts? When we set out to
achieve our goals we have a basic understanding of what is
needed. Granted, we do not actually know what is in store,
but we have a fair and reasonable idea.

Growing up, we were always encouraged by our parents to
believe that we could achieve all we set out to do. The only
thing that would get in our way was our own thinking.

Sometime back, a friend of a friend was spending a lot of
time at our place. Andrew (not his real name) was doing
nothing but blame everybody else for where he was in his
life. Andrew had a marriage break-up; he decided to go on
an overseas holiday, only to find out that the problems he

thought he was leaving behind were still well and truly with him. He came back to nothing, as he'd sold it all to go on his trip. He relocated to another state to 'get it all together', only to have it all fall apart once again. He moved back to his original town to try and give it another go. He entered another relationship that fell apart, then he started the 'dream job', which quickly lost its attraction once he saw that a lot of hard work was required. Now here he was, sitting in my lounge room telling me all this and blaming everybody else for his outcome. I could see his problem staring me right in the face. It was him. Andrew had moved his goal posts.

As things get tough for us, we all have a tendency to want to take the easy way out. The problem here is that every time we take the easy option, we lose out on the lessons that we would have learnt if we'd taken the harder option, the option that would have made us stronger and wiser and better able to handle the same (or even different) problems and issues further down the track. Every time Andrew ran from his problems and issues, he created a reaction that eventually formed a habit.

Blaming other people for our situations is easy; in reality, it's too easy. The people we blame are not going to help us get out of our situations. We have to do that ourselves.

The whole reason for setting standards and goals is to have something to aim at. If we keep moving the goal posts, all it does is confuse us. Sure, we might achieve a few of our aims, but by the time we get to the middle of our lives we will have become frustrated with where and who we are.

My brother Dean is a good example of keeping your eyes firmly planted on your goals and keeping the goal post secured.

When Dean left school, he decided that he would like to get into landscaping and got a job with a local landscape business. Over the years, he proved himself a very competent landscaper. Like me, Dean liked the idea of working for himself, and in 1993 started his own landscape company, Rolling Stone Landscapes.

Dean saw a big hole in the landscape industry where things were not being done all that well, large home landscaping jobs worth over $600 000. Having just started out, he was in no position to start working on jobs involving 215 hectares. He knew that one day he would fulfil those early dreams, if and only if he kept his eyes fixed on that goal.

The biggest reason a lot of us move our goal posts is because we become impatient. Setting a goal, setting your standards is the easy part—on paper. What Dean knew was that one day he would like to be landscaping big properties.

I know for a fact there was no phone call from a wealthy client on the first day of business asking Rolling Stone Landscapes to start landscaping their 2.5 hectares. Dean would have to put in the hard work and learn all the tricks of his trade before he was anywhere near performing a job on that scale. Did he give up after his first day? No.

Today, nine years later, Rolling Stone Landscape jobs have graced the covers of many landscape and prestige homes magazines. Dean is the youngest board member of the Landscape Contractors Association of New South Wales, and his business is highlighted on national television shows.

What is so different about Dean? Easy; he knew his goals, set his standards, focused on his goal posts and no matter how

long, how hard he had to work at it, he was going to finish
what he had started.

We all have small, medium and big goals. There is no way
under the sun that you will ever achieve your biggest goals
unless you have fulfilled the smallest ones.

Over the years, I have been approached by various people
with an idea for a business who wanted me to give them some
guidance. I am, to this day, dumbfounded by the level of
thinking I sometimes see, people who look at what I have done
with a start-up of $50 and automatically think that they
should be able to do the same thing. Please do not get me
wrong. I wish them all the luck in the world, but I created my
own luck. There is no secret formula to what I have done.

Just because someone else achieves something does not
mean that you or I will have the same level of success.

We all have hidden talents within us. The whole process of
achieving your goals is to bring those talents to the surface.
Some people who have sat in my office have already spent the
money that they think they are going to make. That would be
great in an unrealistic world, but they have missed the whole
point. When a little bit of success comes our way, we seem to
think that we are closer to the ultimate goals we have set out
in our lives. When in reality we are only one step closer than
before we started.

If you are guilty of moving your goal posts to achieve
something, you have to ask yourself, have I really achieved
anything? Do not go through your life short-changing yourself
and underestimating your abilities. Stay focused and determined that you will reach your goals.

be the driver

5

WHEN YOU CONTROL THE BALL YOU CONTROL THE SCORE

© Attitude Inc.®

Are you driving yourself to achieve your goals, or are you a passenger hoping that one day you will get there? You need to make a choice—which of these options will you take?

Being creatures of habit, we tend to go through our lives doing many things the same way. We get out of bed and get ready for work the same way, we drive to work using the same roads, we may even clean the house room by room the same way each week. That is fine for getting ready for work, driving to work, or cleaning your house; what is not so fine is that many of us try to achieve our goals and dreams the same way, using the same habits with the same results year after year.

Some of us become programmed to falling short and form habits in this area of our lives. We just accept that we may fail, so we only try a little bit. If we do achieve a goal it's a bonus. We tend to get shocked when something actually happens. Some people would have a heart attack if they achieved their goals and dreams because they have never actually thought they would succeed. They have programmed themselves to fail. Their drive is in neutral.

EVERY NOW AND THEN, BREAK A HABIT

Statistics tell us that it takes a minimum of three weeks to form a habit. My challenge to you as you read this chapter is to break the habits that keep you from achieving all you can.

Dreams and goals are great in writing, either in your diary or on your wall, and we all need to have our goals written down. Wouldn't it be a lot better though, if instead of reading your list of goals every morning you were living some of them? Sounds like pie in the sky? Well, it will be until you take control and become the driver in your quest to reach those goals. It isn't that hard to turn around your thinking and set habits. All it requires is a bit of effort in changing your thought processes and in turn forming a new habit, one that pushes and forces you along your way to completing those goals. There may be a bit of pain involved in changing those habits, but if it only takes *three weeks* to form new and positive habits that will put you back on track towards those goals and dreams you had years ago, wouldn't it be worth it?

Understand your destination

I believe the main reason for falling short of reaching what we want out of life is our lack of understanding of what it is that really drives us. We fall into three categories: those who are driven to succeed, those who are driven to fail and those who put up with whatever they are handed out. The difference between successful people, those who don't bother trying to achieve their goals and those who just take what they can get, is that successful people are driven by success and everything that accompanies it. They understand that success brings with it more opportunities, opportunities which can drive them closer to their goals and dreams.

Please let me explain one very major point. When I talk about successful people, I am not necessarily talking about wealthy people. Being rich does not mean you are successful. I recently met a woman who had decided at a late stage of her life that she would like to train street kids to better their situations and find a job. There was no glamour, no money and no recognition for what she set out to do, but simply by being driven to achieve, she had become successful in making a difference to those lives she came in contact with.

By definition, success is actually achieving what we set out to do, that is, reaching our goals. Whether it is finishing a course to better our career path, or fulfilling a specific goal, it doesn't matter, as long as we are driven to complete what we set out to do.

I know a lot of wealthy people who are absolutely miserable. Sure, they have achieved a lot to be in the financial position they are in today, but in focusing on the dollars they have lost sight of their original goals and dreams.

We have all heard stories about people who have given up their big jobs, some even giving away all their money, and going to work in a third-world country to make a difference. I am yet to meet anyone who can look at a $100 note and laugh. Money will not make you happy, but it can be instrumental in helping you achieve your dreams, which in turn will bring happiness into your life. Just making money with no real reason behind it will only bring emptiness.

In this chapter, I want to take you on a journey that will help you re-think why and how you do what you do and what you actually want out of life.

It sounds so simple, some say too simple, but we all need to re-focus on what we actually wanted out of our lives years ago. A lot of us do re-visit those memories every now and again, but they tend to be just fleeting thoughts that we quickly dismiss. If we aren't driven by those goals and heading in their direction, we will easily lose sight of our original destination. This is the principal key that I have adopted and used in growing Attitude Inc.® from $50 to where it is today.

What is drive? Drive is the factor in each of us that can either get us to our goals or delay us from achieving them. It is the effort that we put into something. Unfortunately, most of our effort, by default, goes into why we can't reach our goals. We try too hard to rationalise the whole process, talking and thinking our way out of reaching anything except mediocrity. You need to swing your effort towards those goals.

START DRIVING YOUR THINKING, ACTIONS AND DECISIONS TOWARDS YOUR DREAMS

How driven are you? When you face hurdles and obstacles in your life, do you continue on your way regardless of the opposition, or do you resign yourself to the fact that it is time to give up? We are all driven, whether it is to succeed in business, find a better job or even create a better environment for our families. The trouble is that a lot of us seem to lose sight along the way of what it was we were aiming at in the first place.

Imagine watching an archery competition where there were no targets. All you have to do is shoot an arrow somewhere, anywhere. That is how some of us attempt to reach our goals. We just aim at any old where, hoping that we are heading in the right direction. Just as in an archery competition, we need to stop, take aim, concentrate and then shoot towards our target. You will be amazed at the results when you actually have something to aim at.

Don't be a passenger

Sometimes we allow other people to take over the controls on our dreams and goals. By now you could probably predict that I am a useless passenger in a car. I may well be the world's worst back-seat driver. It never ceases to amaze me, however, just how many people would rather be passengers on the journey to achieve their goals, and allow people around them to dictate their direction.

The problem with that is twofold.

1. As soon as we let someone else drive our dreams and goals, we are basically handing them the steering rights to our direction.

If I am the driver of my car, I am in control. If there is a corner approaching, it is up to me to steer the car through that corner. It is up to me to take care of the direction. As soon as I become a passenger, I have to put my faith in the driver and hope that they will handle the car in the same manner I would. That is a scary feeling. As a passenger you have surrendered control of your direction.

After one of my speaking engagements I was given a picture produced by the American company Successories®. Still on my wall, it shows a long winding road with the caption 'A bend in the road is not the end of the road, unless you fail to make the turn'. We will all come to bends in our quest to reach our goals. It is only those of us who steer through those bends who will survive another day and be just that little bit closer to achieving our goals.

When I had my motorbike accident, I was a pillion passenger. I surrendered control of that bike to the person steering it. As we were hurtling down the road, I saw what was about to unfold; I could see the car ahead about to do a U-turn. I knew that it was going to hurt, but there was nothing I could do about it. I wasn't steering the direction of that motorbike.

As soon as you allow yourself to let other people take control and set your direction, you have to accept the consequences. Good or bad. You can't blame other people for not reaching your own goals if you were not the one steering—you have handed them the controls.

2. *You never get to appreciate what you have or where you have come from.*

My wife comes from another state. Every now and then we make the trek north to catch up with her relatives. As I love driving and hate being a passenger, I drive the entire way myself. Vanessa generally sleeps.

Have you ever slept in the car (not while driving, I hope) and when you woke up found yourself in totally new surroundings? The boredom of sitting in the passenger seat with nothing to do is lessened by the fact that you have slept through the trip. Vanessa wakes up every now and then, and all of a sudden (to her) we are in her home state. To her it doesn't feel as though it took long. But the driver (me) knows exactly what it takes to get there. I understand the effort that was required, so as soon as I get out of the car, I can really appreciate what I have achieved, and it is time to relax.

There are some people who would rather sit back and let other people do all the work to get them to where they want to go in life. They want to be passengers on the way to fulfil their own goals. If they ever get what they want out of life, they don't actually appreciate how or why they are there. The feeling of accomplishment is short lived, as they haven't done much along the way.

The journey to reaching our goals and dreams is just as important as the destination. It is what we learn along the way, whether about ourselves or our experiences, that makes the journey worthwhile. In the end you will have a level of appreciation as to how and why you have reached those goals that a passenger will never have.

I used agents to represent my brand in the early years of my business. I liked the concept of agents, as their pay was based on the sales they made. All these agents had their own businesses representing various clothing labels.

A few years after starting my business I made one of my first-ever speaking engagements. Standing around, talking to some of the delegates from the conference afterwards, I was approached by a young man who wanted to discuss something with me. We sat down and he proceeded to ask for a job. He told me where his life was at that time and that he wanted to take control over his future. He was basically discovering the principle of driving his own destiny. Unfortunately there were no jobs available at the time, but a few days later he rang to ask if he could be the agent for my brand in a state where at the time we had no representation.

We had a long discussion. Being an agent is not the easiest of jobs because basically you are running your own business. I told him to go away and really think about it, but he came back saying that he really wanted the opportunity.

He started like wildfire. His sales were unbelievable. I offered him all the help he needed. I flew regularly to meet with him and took him on trips to show him how to get better sales and gave him tips on all the other areas of running his own business. Then I left him to it.

All of a sudden his sales dropped dramatically. He started ringing all the time, wanting me to set up appointments and finish his sales. It seemed that he had given up once he had to get out there and create his own leads and his own opportunities.

He had missed one very important lesson: he needed to take the responsibility for driving towards his own goals and dreams. Because I was driven to succeed I had assumed that he was wired that way as well. After only three months he rang me to ask for a reference saying that he worked as an agent for Attitude Inc.®. I inquired why; he was buying a new car. I knew what his sales were so I knew there was no way he could afford a new car, and a $35 000 one at that.

I spent a long time trying to help him understand that it was a bit early for that type of purchase. He didn't listen and went out and leased the car. The reasoning behind it was that I had a nice car, and if I had a nice car he should have one too. He was fixated on what I had, not on what he wanted out of life or on setting his own goals and achieving them. The car was a short-term fix to make him feel as though he was on his way. He had replaced true success with a feeling of surface success.

About two months later, he rang to tell me he was leaving, to work in a bar. He couldn't afford the car. He had failed to reach his goals so he would work towards an easier set of goals. Work as an agent was a bit hard and he hadn't expected to put in the number of hours required. His problem was that he lacked the drive. He had been a passenger through his short working life. While I was doing most of the work, he excelled. As soon as I let him take control and drive his own future it all fell down. He had been driven by the short term and by appearances, not by what he really wanted out of life.

Map your route

We need to have goals, but we also need a map of how we are going to get there. Short-term solutions will never send us forward; in fact they will send us backwards in the end.

I have just bought a new car which has satellite navigation as a standard feature. All I need to do is program my destination into the unit, and press 'go'; it will work out the best route for me. It has proved to be a valuable tool. Before I bought this car I relied on looking up where I was going in a street directory. On those occasions when I'd accidentally left my street directory at home, I would eventually make it to my destination, but only after stopping numerous times to ask for directions, some of them not that good. With the navigation system in my car it is a lot easier.

Some of us go through our lives with no map to give us directions, hoping that we can make it to our goals by memory alone. We know where we want to end up, but we have no idea how we are going to get there. The preparation involved in mapping out directions, spotting the possible hurdles on the way, that will help us understand what is required.

When you look at a street map, you may see a few one-way streets that you are unable to turn down, forcing you to choose another route. The same principle applies to mapping out your future. When you take the time to carefully choose the best route, you will be able to avoid those issues that would have crossed your path if you weren't prepared, and made your trip a bit longer. We need to programme our goals and dreams into our actions and thinking so that by habit we will be on our way along the road to success. With a properly navigated route, the journey will seem a lot clearer and easier.

The success of the Attitude Inc.® brand, and the range of different products, has led to numerous approaches from people wanting to open up shops stocking only the Attitude Inc.® brand. It seemed an obvious direction for the company to move into.

A young guy who wanted to get away from Sydney to start a new chapter of his life in another state approached me after we had a couple of these stores up and running. He had seen the growth of the brand and the potential in having a store totally devoted to its product range. This business model really appealed to him.

We met on numerous occasions so he could totally understand the range and see if he had what was needed—not from my perspective, but from his. I wanted to be sure that he really wanted to move in this direction. Running a small business is not easy, especially if you have never taken that step before. As we had a company-owned store already in operation, all he had to do was to model his store after ours; he agreed that this was exactly the way he would do it.

Over our many conversations I asked him why he wanted to change the direction of his life. He told me that he had dreams and goals for both himself and his family and he wanted to take control of his direction. He was tired of working for other people and watching them get ahead. He wanted his hard work and effort to pay off for him. He wanted to be the master of his own destiny. He was a driven person who knew exactly what he wanted. Or so he said.

He found a location and set up the shop. It looked great. Every now and then I would fly interstate for business and call in to see how he was going. While the store was doing okay, all too soon I could see he was starting to lose interest. We started getting phone calls from customers complaining about his level of service and lack of product knowledge, and the shop always being closed.

While this wasn't my fault it started to become my problem, as I didn't want anyone to judge my business based on someone else's lack of effort. One day I rang around 3 pm to tell him of a new promotion we were doing through the Attitude stockist network nation-wide, but there was no one there. The next morning I had my secretary follow up on the call. There was still no one there. She finally spoke to him at around lunchtime, when he told her that he was going to open the shop at 10 am and shut at 3 pm every day, as he wanted to spend more time doing the things he liked. Because he owned the business he felt he could do whatever he wanted. True, this was entirely up to him as we were just the supplier of the stock, but it blew me away. He was right. He could do anything he wanted, but when starting a business you need to put in a lot of work and effort to set it up. It is fine to try and live your dreams, but first you need to make sure that those dreams will last a long time, not just for the short term because you lose sight of what you are really trying to achieve and you just live for the now.

Here was a man who only four months earlier I thought had the drive and determination to succeed at anything—and now he had all but given up. When I finally spoke to him he first tried the blame game. It was our fault that the products weren't selling, it was our fault that the products weren't cheaper, etcetera.

I let him waffle for around an hour and then, as I do quite

well, I gave him my opinion. In the first place, products don't just walk off the shelf and sell themselves. That's what a salesperson is there for. To sell! In the second place, you need to let people know you are open. He hadn't advertised, or even put the name of his shop up on the front window. His attitude was also driving customers away. It was quite evident to a lot of people who had walked into his shop that he really didn't want to be there. As for prices, I reminded him of his initial comment months earlier, about how good the price points were on our product range. We were selling extremely well in our own store and in over 1500 stores throughout the country, so I knew price wasn't an issue.

It was such a shame to see this man blame everybody around him for the direction that he himself had taken. No one twisted his arm to make him do what he did. He was the one who approached us. He was the one who wanted to take this path in his life.

I told him that we would buy back the stock so he could go and do something else, if that was what he wanted. I didn't want the hard work that I had put in over six years to be affected by one person's lack of direction. He went back to working for someone else and from what I hear he is still miserable, hating his new job.

You see, while he knew where he wanted to end up, he failed to plan out his quest and look at a map of how he was going to get to his goals. The problem wasn't the products or the operating times or even the prices. It was him, and his thinking! He didn't put action to what he had in his head. The drive that is needed to reach your goals is a most important factor. Without the proper drive, we will all fall short, creating an atmosphere of frustration.

Blame is the sound of surrender and defeat. We will always find people to blame for why we are the way we are, or why we are in the position we are today, but is that going to change our circumstances? It may make us feel a bit better at the time, but it isn't going to solve our problems. As far as this guy was concerned, I was to blame for letting him open a shop. The reality was that his lack of planning and direction was to blame, but he could never see that.

Another mistake some of us make along the road is to look at other people's maps instead of our own. The store owner, and the would-be agent you read about earlier, had both seen what I had achieved and decided that they wanted to go down the same road. That may be the right road for some people, but you need to be certain that it really is the right path and direction for you. Never simply copy someone else's direction. What is successful for one may be a disaster for you. Each of us has different goals, so the maps we need to look at will obviously be different.

Imagine trying to find your way around the streets of New York using a map of London. You would find out fairly quickly that it isn't working. Why then take other people's directions to achieve your goals?

Fuel

What fuels your drive? As you read earlier, I have just bought a new car. I can only use the highest grade of unleaded fuel if it is to perform at its peak. If I decide to put diesel fuel into the tank, I will feel the effects of that bad choice in a matter of minutes, if not seconds. The fuel that you direct into your drive will result either in the desired outcomes, or in falling short of achieving what you set out to do.

What do I mean when I talk about fuel? I mean many things—what do you read for instance? Is it literature that will challenge your thinking and create an atmosphere of excellence?

Who are your friends? Do they continually tell you that you can't achieve anything, or do you have people around you who push you towards your goals and dreams?

How is your thinking? Do you just accept defeat, or are you determined that even if some things slow you down, you will reach your goals no matter what?

WHAT WE LET INTO OUR THINKING CAN AND WILL AFFECT OUR DRIVE

Being mentally prepared is great, but we also need to be physically prepared for the challenges that approach. Many of us get our heads in order, but we seem to neglect our physical bodies. The more energy we have, the longer and harder we will be able to work towards completing those goals. Being physically and mentally prepared will save you a lot of time and effort.

Let's illustrate this another way: if you were to enter a marathon, you would prepare yourself not only by training your body; you would also adjust your diet, adjust your thinking and adjust your surroundings. You wouldn't train every day at the gym and on the track and then go home and eat junk food. You would have to focus on every part of your training so that you could use each one as fuel.

The same principle applies to reaching your goals. You need to fuel those desires by taking on a total approach.

Be determined that you will be the driver of your life. Don't accept other people trying to take control over your dreams and goals. If you find you are heading down a path that is taking you away from what you want, just turn around and head in the proper direction. We will all make mistakes at different times in our lives. The key to being successful is not to make the same mistake too often.

wake up and start
dreaming

6

DON'T FOLLOW YOUR DREAMS . . .
LET THEM FOLLOW YOU

The theme of this chapter goes hand in hand with the chapter you have just read on drive. Our dreams and aspirations will always remain out of reach unless we have the drive and determination to fulfil them. But we have to have the dream in the first place . . . if we have nothing to drive ourselves toward, we will end up like a car stuck on a roundabout when its driver has no idea how to get off. By the time you finish this chapter, I hope to have totally changed your thinking and understanding on reaching your dreams.

We all have dreams. I don't mean the ones we have when we are asleep, I mean the dreams and goals that we want to make a reality. Whether it is owning a house, buying a nice car, going on a holiday with our family once a year, or even spending more time with our loved ones, we all have dreams.

The problem is, as we go through our lives we lose sight of those dreams; too often we end up just existing, or even just surviving, doing things that don't excite us.

You need to apply determination to achieving those goals and dreams. Determination is a factor that lets a lot of us down in our journey towards completing those goals. Keeping mind, heart and soul focused on the end result will play a big part in actually getting there. When you are determined that nothing is going to slow you down or stop you achieving what you set out to do, you will automatically break down some of the mental obstacles that might hinder you.

Let me give you an example. Let's say you're a bit over-weight. I know how that feels—I was a bit of a tubby when I was younger. If you are determined to change yourself, your body shape, your weight, you have made your brain respond to your body's needs. When you go to the gym, the mindset is already there, because you have decided that this is part of the process needed to reach your goal. It isn't the most pleasant experience trying to lose weight, but once you start to see some results, you become even more determined to lose more. Without determination, you would probably give up early on, maybe not even start; you would be listening to reasons for putting it off, or why you don't really need to lose those 'cuddly' bulges.

The key to living a fulfilled life is to make your dreams a living reality, like my friend Luke. Over lunch recently, he was telling me about a dream that is now almost a reality. As a child growing up in Papua New Guinea, the day a helicopter landed on the school oval Luke decided right then and there that one day he would get his helicopter pilot's licence. Now I know nearly all of us have wanted to be a pilot, a fireman or a racecar driver at one stage, but Luke has kept that dream alive ever since. He started a business years ago with one result in mind—get it running well so he could fund his pilot's licence fees. Last year he worked on the theory courses every weekend; that way he could still concentrate on his business during the week. This year he worked his business so well that he was able to take two days off a week to do the practical courses. At the time of writing, Luke was only two weeks away from getting his helicopter pilot's licence. Luke's dream of years ago took hard work and effort to achieve, he may even have put it on the back-burner for a while, but he remained determined that he would reach his goal one day.

One of the traps on the way to success is getting caught up with what everybody else is doing instead of with what we want to achieve. When you are focused on other people's success all the time, you are taking your eyes off your own goals and dreams—and that means you lose all direction towards reaching your own goals.

One of the biggest mistakes you can make is to measure your own success, and your progress, against other people's. What is good for them, and how they have achieved and reached their own dreams and goals, is not normally how it will work for you. Additionally, copying other people may mean you do not enjoy the actual process as much. It is the journey that makes the end result so worthwhile.

If you are getting nowhere as you try to reach your goals, and you are starting to get frustrated, perhaps you need to turn your thinking around and look at your situation from a totally different direction. Stop looking at your goals from the direction you have been viewing them for the past however many years. You may need to adjust your thinking. Don't accept negative thoughts ('I'm never going to get there'). The day you believe such thoughts is the day you become stagnant.

Enjoy your successes

Sadly, the 'tall poppy syndrome' is alive and well in today's climate. There are always people out there just waiting to pull successful people down to their level. If you are on your way to achieving your goals or living one of your dreams, make sure you enjoy every minute of the process. Don't complicate your thinking so much that you feel guilty when you actually reach one of your goals. Be proud of it; shout it from the rooftops. Isn't that what we all want in our lives, to achieve our goals? And remember, while there may be some who will try to pull you down, there are many more who will be encouraged by your success. Make sure you share your success with those around you.

If you've achieved all of your goals and dreams, you could just skip the rest of this chapter and go on to the next one. Before you do, though, I challenge you: set yourself new goals. This time, make them bigger, and harder to reach. But if you take up my challenges, like me, who still has a few dreams to reach, you will need to start preparing yourself and your thinking for a radical change.

'Dream psychology'

I want to share with you 'dream psychology', a technique I used in fulfilling one of my own personal goals. It may sound simplistic, but by changing my thinking and using the method I'm now going to talk about, I was able to take my business from a $50 company to a multimillion-dollar company—all through focusing on a dream that had nothing to do with my business.

Through sharing this story, I trust that you will see how easy it is to actually reach those goals once you clear your head of the negative mindsets and old thinking that have been cluttering it for years.

Just before I started Attitude Inc.® in 1995 I was working at a health and fitness centre. While I quite enjoyed my job, I was getting more and more frustrated with not actually achieving anything. By that I mean, sure I was getting paid, and yes, I had progressed up the ladder to manager, but those dreams that I had from when I was younger were still so far off I couldn't see them, let alone plan for them.

In 1995 I had come to a point where the only way that I could actually start living my dreams was to take the responsibility and risk of getting myself there. This might sound like common sense, but there are many people out there who will always fall short of their goals because they are waiting for them to 'just happen', for someone to hand them their lifelong dream on a golden platter. It won't happen!

From an early age I had one big dream. I wanted a nice car. That was it. As I worked at the gym I saw my dream car getting further and further away; the funny thing was, I was starting to accept, in my thinking and my actions, that it would never be. I wasn't earning nearly enough money there to make that dream a reality, I had all but given up on it. I could have continued with different jobs and reached that goal 'one day', but I was impatient, I wanted it now. It came to me that I had to do something about it. And just at that point, the woman at my church (the one who gave me a talking-to about my 'attitude problem') provided the final push for change. I decided to stop accepting the ordinary and have a go at achieving the extra-ordinary. I really had nothing to lose. Now I didn't know how I would go, but I had to give it my best shot.

Many people never attempt to reach their dreams or goals because they are scared they won't make it, or because they seem so far out of their grasp that they give up in their thinking before they even start. I believe we can't just live ordinary lives doing ordinary things hoping to achieve ordinary goals—we all need to step out and try living extra-ordinary lives. (By 'extra-ordinary' I mean 'out of line ordinary; exceptional'; I don't mean 'extraordinary' as in 'odd'.) Whatever you do, do it with an attitude of being extra-ordinary, going that extra distance, doing that little bit more than you would normally have done.

What are your dreams? Don't say, to be 'successful', or to 'own a business'. Those are just the results or outcomes of reaching your dreams.

WHAT DREAMS DID YOU HAVE TEN YEARS AGO? HAVE YOU REACHED ANY OF THOSE YET?

What are the dreams that you have actually had for years? Why do you want them? Think back, maybe even to when you were still in school. Owning a house? Having a holiday every year? Spending more time with your family?

Don't think for a minute that just because you were young and had some big and stupid dreams that they don't matter now. They do. Remember Luke and his helicopter? I believe that in our younger years we focus on the dreams of what will really make us happy. When we get older (and some say wiser) we tend to complicate our thoughts and situations by trying to rationalise everything.

Starting my business was hard; for two years I worked a part-time job and put every bit of capital into the business. I had one dream and one dream only at that time, and that was to have a nice car. I have spoken on this subject a lot at conferences and seminars, and I am still confronted by people who think that I focused on the car instead of my business. My response to that is simple. The business was and still is the driving factor in my desire to achieve my dream. Now I have more goals and dreams, and my business is the financier of those goals.

It was the simplicity of that dream which helped take my company to where it is today.

Let me explain. I didn't think about buying that car on the first day. I knew that to make my dream a reality I needed to grow my business, and if I grew my business enough I could get my nice car. Simple. You see, owning a successful business was a by-product of aiming at reaching my dream.

Too often, however, we complicate our dreams by rationalising our thinking to a lower standard. Why focus just on the success of something if there is nothing else to show for it, and your dream is further away than when you started? If your ultimate dream is to own your house, then all you need to concentrate on is how are you going to achieve that. If it is by getting a better paying job or starting your own business, go and do it. Don't sit there for years thinking about it. There is no point slaving for years on end, moving up the corporate ladder only to end up burnt-out and miserable, if you have nothing to show for it. You need to re-focus on reaching those lifelong dreams.

The car that I had when I started Attitude Inc.® was a little hatchback. I carried all my stock with me around to the shops and if you have ever owned a little hatchback, you would understand that there isn't much room in them at all. It really didn't suit what I was trying to achieve. I never lost sight of my ultimate dream, however. Three-and-a-half years after I started my business I was able to buy a new car. I had made one of my dreams a reality.

LIKE CLAY THAT IS SHAPED INTO A PIECE OF ART, SO OUR DREAMS HAVE TO BE SHAPED

You would think that right at the point of making your dreams come true you would be happy. I was, but I was also fretting. Going through my head were thoughts like 'what would happen if I couldn't afford the car in six months' time?' and 'what happens if I am making the wrong decision?' But those nervous thoughts actually helped me learn a simple but effective lesson. At one point or another we all seem to try and talk ourselves out of achieving what we set out to do in the first place. Our thinking tends to keep us in a safe environment. It isn't until we learn to step out of that safe environment that we will achieve greater things.

I made the decision the day I bought the car that the only way to take away the feelings of the 'what ifs' was to make my business bigger so I wouldn't have a problem paying for the car. Within two months the 'what if' thoughts had gone. The business was stronger and now so much bigger that any thought of not being able to afford the car was forgotten. I was on cloud nine for months. I achieved more from buying that car than I had ever imagined. In three years I had taken my thinking from sitting in a gym office and never being able to reach my dreams to sitting in a $40 000 car and owning a company with national coverage.

Now that I had reached that dream, I decided I wanted more of the same. I didn't want my level of dreaming to stop there. So I had another dream, a better car. Within a year I was sitting in the sales office of the car yard, with the same 'what ifs' running through my head. 'What if I can't afford it in six months' time?' I got the car and that day again determined to grow the business so that keeping the car would not be an issue. Sure enough the business grew. Every time I decided to live one of my dreams it forced my business to grow by making me expand my thinking.

It is odd, but as soon as we achieve a dream or goal we all tend to talk ourselves out of why we should have it. I have had numerous cars in the years since then, and my business has continued to grow because of one simple point. I wanted a bigger and better dream. My business was the means of making that simple dream become a reality. I had to learn a lot about growing my business, and I definitely had to learn to be a good businessman, but I knew from day one what it was I was trying to achieve.

Don't over-complicate what you want out of your life, your dreams. Just aim at them and utilise everything around you to achieve them. What is your means for making your dreams become reality? Will your job do it, or do you need to re-evaluate where you are headed and take control of your own destiny? Making money in itself should never be your dream. It is what that money will bring you that will make your dreams and goals become reality. When you focus on the money, you are leaving yourself open to disappointment if for some unfore-seen reason your finances suffer a hiccup. Too many people get caught by this, by the thought that being rich will bring them happiness and everything they wanted. Until you actually know what your dreams are, all the money in the world will amount to nothing.

Many business owners have told me why they originally started their own business. Most often it was for a reason like spending more time with their families, or going on holidays more regularly, simple dreams. So often, however, they get so caught up in keeping the business going that they lose sight of the reason, the actual dream behind starting that business in the first place. Please do not misunderstand me. I am not saying that owning a business doesn't require a lot of time and effort. It is just that so often we become so involved in the thing that was supposed to help us live our dream that we move in the opposite direction, away from the dream.

We need to remain focused on our dreams 100 per cent of the time. You will see that the more you stay focused, the easier it becomes to make decisions within your business or per-sonal life, because these decisions now have a direct result on achieving your dreams and goals. Positioning your dreams as the eventual outcome makes decision-making a lot easier.

I view our dreams and goals as our life's business plan. Most businesses have a business plan. In that plan we set out what we hope to achieve in our business for that year or for years to come. When you focus on your dreams and goals as life's business plan, you will see more easily what is required to reach those dreams.

Take some risks

To move closer to your goals and dreams, you are going to have to take some risks. I don't mean go out there and ruin everything you have worked for, but take calculated risks. Stepping out and doing something that you haven't tried, or even thought of before, may turn out to be the biggest key to unlocking those dreams.

When I first started Attitude Inc.® I took a risk. I have had some people say to me I had nothing to lose, 'it was only $50'. But it was the only $50 I had. If I lost that $50 because of a bad business decision, I would be left with nothing again. The risk I took seven years ago turned my life around to a point where I have fulfilled one of my biggest dreams. The simple action of taking that risk proved the biggest key to where I am today.

Too often we blow off the small decisions in our lives because we are waiting for the 'big ones' to come along and change everything for us. Most risks we take, which on the outside seem at the time to be huge, in reality are quite small. To get closer to living your dreams and achieving your goals you are going to have to decide that you will take some calculated risks from today on. If you want that better job so you can spend time with your family, you will need to take a risk and apply for that job. You may have to give up the security of your current employment but just think of the reward when that risk pays off and you are spending that extra time with your family. If you want to start your own business so you can pay your house off and go on a holiday every year, you need to go start that business and stop putting the decision off. You need to do the research for your products, you need to find the location, and you need to get up, step out and take the risk. But you need to be smart about it at the same time.

I would have never bought that first car if I couldn't afford it—but I had to stop and look at my dreams from a different angle.

Have you ever been faced with a huge problem? A problem which at the time seemed huge, impossible to work out, but which as soon as you slept on it or got someone else's opinion you started to see in a clearer light?

It is the same with your dreams. You need to stop and look at them from a different direction. When you do that you will be able to assess what risks you need to take; that way you won't just jump in and potentially fall short, only to disappoint yourself.

Sacrifice

I've spoken of sacrifice earlier. To reach your dreams and goals you will eventually have to sacrifice something, perhaps many things. It might be your current direction, some of your friends or even your time. It still amazes me the way some people think they are going to get everything they want out of life by staying the same person or doing the same thing day after day. They are relying on others to make the sacrifices for them.

There aren't any short-cuts to reaching your goals or living your dreams. I received a fax one day that I have kept because I was so blown away by its contents. This is how it read:

Dear Mr Herald,

I am writing to you today to ask a favour.

I have been on an overseas holiday for the past 8 months and I have just returned to Australia.

As I have been away for so long I have not had a full-time job, and because of this my funds have all dried up.

I was writing this fax to ask if you would consider giving me $36 000.00. This is how I will spend the money.

$8750.00—to pay off credit card debt

$5500.00—to repay my parents

$15 000.00—to buy a car

$6750.00—to go on a trip around Australia.

Please feel free to call me and I will let you know the account for the money to be transferred into.

Surely this was a joke. I faxed the letter back with a note on the bottom saying 'Love to give you the money, please call me at my office'. I wanted to see what this was all about. About 30 minutes later my secretary came into my office to tell me that the man who wrote the fax was on the phone and it was definitely no joke. Picking up the phone, I could tell that the man at the other end was all excited. I asked him why he would think I would pay for his expenses. He proceeded to tell me that he was hoping one day someone would just give him the money, no questions asked, as he didn't want to waste the time doing it himself. I will just say that our conversation ended there.

This man failed to realise that to get anywhere in life we need to sacrifice. His sacrifice would have been to go to work to afford all those things for himself, instead of expecting other people to fulfil his dreams.

Focus

The biggest reason we miss out on reaching our dreams is that we don't focus on them hard enough. Once we let them out of our sight we tend to forget them. You need to keep those dreams and goals close to you so you can see them. I knew the car that I wanted because every now and then I would focus on it in my mind.

Now I couldn't go and buy it right then, but I knew one day I would. Keeping it always within focus, always in my thinking, actually brought the whole dream a lot closer.

KEEPING YOUR DREAMS AND GOALS WITHIN FOCUS MEANS THEY ARE WITHIN YOUR REACH

What was it years ago that you dreamed of having or being? Where was it that you dreamed of going? Do you remember? If you can't, then you've lost your focus, and that's why you haven't achieved those aspirations.

What is it that you do focus on? Is it the reasons why you will never make it to your goals and dreams? If that's where you focus, the only thing you can blame at the end of your life for not reaching your dreams and goals is your thinking. I know that it is easy to focus on the negative all the time; our minds and thinking are somehow wired that way.

One key to reaching your dreams is changing your focus. You need to start acknowledging that you *can* make it, that you *can* achieve those dreams and goals. The day you determine to yourself that you are going to focus your attention and efforts on achieving those goals is the day that you will get closer to that final achievement.

Our younger daughter has just gone through the learning-how-to-walk stage. It is the funniest thing to watch. Obviously I can't remember what it was like when I was her age, but I have my own slant on it. I can just imagine Brooke looking at my wife and me walking around everywhere and knowing that she wants to do that too. So up she gets, she tries a couple of steps and bang, onto the floor she falls. It takes her many attempts and a lot of falls until she masters that skill.

You too will fall over a lot of times on your way to reaching your dreams and goals. How focused you are on trying to reach them will determine how successful you are. Walking can only be mastered one step at a time. Remember, with my car, I had to take one step at a time before I was anywhere near reaching my dream.

Too many times we frustrate ourselves by wanting it now. If we can't have it now then we don't want it. I know, because I used to be like that. But there is another way. I call it the lay-by principle. When I met my wife she was right into lay-bys. She had it all planned out. Every week she would pay a bit off here, a bit off there. After a few weeks (or months) she would make the last payment and it was hers. I didn't understand the concept at first. I always wanted it now, or not at all. I was impatient. Fortunately for me, I came to understand!

When we become impatient with our dreams and goals, we have a tendency to either cut corners or give up entirely. But we need to have that lay-by mentality. If we work at it bit by bit, week after week, eventually it will be ours for the taking.

Don't change your aim

The final point in this chapter is a warning. Don't change your dreams and goals. You can add to them, but you can never take them away. As soon as you allow yourself to change your dreams you need to change your direction. It is all too easy to give up on some dreams, the hardest ones, the goals so big that you cannot comprehend that you will ever reach them. But in changing them or forgetting about them you set your thinking backwards. I had a big 'stupid' goal when I first started Attitude Inc.®. Retire by the time I was 31. This is the silly goal, the dream you just throw in there at the time. You never think you'll make it but you put it in there anyway.

In 2001 when I licensed Attitude Inc.® totally, I effectively 'retired' from the day-to-day running of the company. I still own the company and play a major role in its direction, but I have actually achieved what I set out to do. If I had allowed negative thinking to get the better of me, I would have given up on that line of thought and missed out on a huge change in my lifestyle and direction.

So don't change your goals no matter how big or, in your eyes, how 'stupid' they are. One day you may reach them and who knows, if you apply what you have just read, it could be a lot sooner than you originally thought.

opportunity is knocking | 7 |

7

OBSTACLES ARE WHAT YOU SEE WHEN YOU TAKE YOUR EYES OFF THE GOAL

© Attitude Inc.®

Many, many people fail to get ahead in life, or to change the wrong direction they are heading in, because they do not recognise the great opportunities that come their way on a regular basis. We are all faced with different opportunities each day. If we only knew how to identify them, we would save ourselves a lot of time and misused effort.

Many of us fail to recognise that great opportunities are there to be acted on. Acting on an opportunity, whether it's big or small, will help us get to our goal a lot quicker, whether it is buying a house, spending more time with the family or choosing a career path. All of us have one thing in common—opportunities will at some point come our way. The difference between us is that some of us will see the opportunities presenting themselves, and some of us will let them pass by without even realising they were there.

Life is a race—not a short sprint, but a gruelling marathon. It is tough and it is hard, but it is how you approach it that will inevitably lead to success or frustration.

I was at my older daughter's athletics carnival one day, watching the different races unfold. They started with the 50-metre sprints, where those involved went out hard and fast as soon as the starter's gun was fired.

Then came the time for the 800-metre race. The participants lined up at the starting line, and 'bang', off they went. Almost half the racers went out as fast as they could. About halfway through, they started to get tired, as their energy had all but run out. Those who started off more slowly caught up, and then went past, leading by a long way. Remember, if you go out hard and fast towards your goals, you will need to ensure you have the energy and the sticking power to keep going.

Some of the opportunities that come your way might be disguised as impossible situations; not all great opportunities look and smell like roses. Spotting them isn't that easy. Remember, life isn't easy. If it was, we would all be doing extremely well at everything we put our hands to.

One of my sayings (which has aggravated my friends for years) is, 'I don't have problems, I have opportunities'. When you face a problem in your life, do you give up and think the worst, or do you see that problem as an opportunity to change your situation? Do you focus on the problem, or do you look for what the outcome could be if you changed your focus?

A lot of us miss opportunities that come our way because we are waiting for the proverbial 'pot of gold at the end of the rainbow' scenario to come our way.

A friend in the record industry told me recently a story about the world-famous pop group, the Beatles. Did you know that a record company knocked back the opportunity to sign the Beatles, because they 'didn't like their sound'? What a missed opportunity that was! Imagine being that record company when the Beatles were at the height of their popularity. They must have been kicking themselves.

Not all opportunities come in the shape you might expect. They can come disguised in many forms—someone you meet, being in the right place at the right time . . . just about anything. What opportunities have you let slip by? We have all missed opportunities in our lives, things we regret not doing, not taking up, not completing. The key is to learn from those experiences, and determine to look at every opportunity while it is still within reach. What you then need to do is act wisely and sensibly on that opportunity. You never know—if you let it slip, it might be a long time before another one comes your way.

I was sitting in my office one day when my secretary buzzed through that a woman on the phone just 'had' to talk to me. I took the call, from a woman who had seen me interviewed on a current affairs programme and liked how I had made the most out of the opportunities that came across my path. She wanted direction for her life.

I have always made myself available to help other small business operators. When I first started, no one I contacted for advice wanted to give me the time of day, so I determined early on that I would help as many people as I could. It's not that I thought I knew it all, just that I wanted to assist people who were in the same situation as I was when I started.

Sitting in my office a few days later, Susan started to tell me of where her life was now and what she wanted to do about it. She was tired of being a stay-at-home mum now her children had all started school; the boredom was eating away at her.

We spoke for quite some time about what I had done to change my situation, what it actually took, then I told her to go away and think of what she wanted to do. About a month later Susan came back to my office all excited. She had designed a range of products aimed at new mothers that were totally different to anything then on the market. When I saw her concepts, I knew straightaway that she was on a real winner. She had researched the marketplace and found a niche. She showed me the drawings of her concepts; she had fabrics, colours and styles already picked out. It seemed she had seen a new direction for her life and was going to get there no matter what. We agreed that we would meet every week until she was confident she was able to go it alone.

I organised manufacturers for her, even set up appointments with major retail outlets. Within a couple of months she had the finished samples; they were fantastic. We organised for a few mothers to come in and look at the samples. Every single mother wanted to order one or more of Susan's products on the spot.

Susan's excitement, the change in her outlook on life was worth all the effort. She had changed from someone with a jaundiced, disillusioned outlook to someone who had the drive and the passion to make a success of her new business.

Susan's first appointment with one of the major retailers was set for the following week. She came to my office, wanting to go over a few things so she was clear in her own thinking. We talked for a while, and then came to the pricing of the products. Going through them, item by item, I was shocked, to say the least. I knew exactly how much each one cost to make, having been involved in the whole process from day one. Susan had marked up each design by at least 1000 per cent. Yes, you read it right the first time, 1000 per cent. I was stunned. I quizzed her on the issue, and she told me that she and her husband had discussed it and wanted to make as much profit as they could, in the quickest time possible.

I have always been one for making a profit, but I have never subscribed to the 'grab the cash and run' theory. Now I don't claim to be a business guru, but I do understand pricing yourself out of the marketplace. We had to agree to disagree on the pricing issue—she wouldn't even contemplate a different point of view—and she went on her way.

I rang Susan a while later to see how it was all going. She had orders from three of the major retailers, totalling 1000 units each of the four styles in her range.

I was so happy for her. Then came the crunch. Because of the price that she was selling them for, each and every one of the retailers had ordered 'sale or return'. This basically means that if the retailer doesn't sell the items they don't pay for them. I have never adopted that method in my business, as there is really no incentive for a retailer to sell a product if they can just give it back, but as long as Susan was confident that it was going to work, she was well on her way to reaching her goals. It was not my position to try and change her mind. It was her dream that she was trying to bring into reality. We will come back to Susan a little later.

When opportunities come our way, what we make of them determines how fast we get to our ultimate goal.

The 3 A's of opportunity

I believe there are three simple words you need to keep in mind when it comes to making the most out of the opportunities that present themselves. They are:

1. Anticipation
2. Action
3. Awareness

These three words can be the keys to eliminating the frustrating thought patterns that have kept you missing opportunities.

Anticipation

The dictionary's meaning for anticipation is 'to realise beforehand; foretaste or foresee'.

A lot of people seem to do nothing but anticipate dramas. They become so used to living with what they get that they just expect more of the same. They start seeing problems before a problem actually exists; in reality they probably wouldn't have a problem if they hadn't thought it into existence. Every day, it seems, there is a new drama to talk about. The reason is easy. They have programmed their minds and their thinking to anticipate problems and to accept that those problems are there to stay. If you have this outlook on life you need to change your mindset to one of positivity.

What is the worst that could happen if you changed your thinking? Start to anticipate good opportunities coming your way. Until you change the thought processes regarding your own life, and ensure that you are the one holding the strings, nothing will change. What do you 'just accept' in your life? What aren't you happy with? What have you wanted to change about yourself or your situation, maybe for a long time? Have you just kept on putting it off? Change it. No, it's not pie in the sky thinking; all you have to do is focus your thoughts, and in turn your actions, on the good stuff instead of the dramas.

When Susan came into my office, she was sick and tired of the way that she was just existing. Her life seemed to be set on cruise control. She wanted to make a change and for the better. And by wanting that change for herself, she was already anticipating that change was needed. It is rare for new opportunities to just fall in our laps. If and when they do, they seem to go as quickly as they came. We all know the saying 'easy come, easy go'. Susan made the difference in her life by taking back control.

When my daughter Jade was a bit younger she went through a period in which she experienced growing pains, as we all have. As her body was preparing for a growth spurt she literally felt the effects of that process. There were some nights when she was reduced to tears by the pain that accompanied the change that was needed. Why is it that when we start to focus on personal growth we don't expect any 'pain' to accompany the process? That 'pain' is needed for us to grow through situations and circumstances, and overall will elevate us to a new level of thinking, and ultimately new ways of reacting to opportunities. Sometimes we will need to change things about ourselves before we will be able to see the opportunities in front of us; you might be amazed at how clearly you will identify those opportunities.

The reason I had only $50 in the bank at the age of 25 was that I couldn't handle my money. What do you think was the biggest change I had to make as my business took off? My business style? No. My people skills? No. (Depends who you ask.) It was my attitude towards money. As long as I didn't address this issue, no matter how much I turned over in my business, I was going to end up back in the same position. Once I took steps to eradicate this pitfall, I was able to see the opportunities around me for what they really were. It is amazing what little changes you actually need to make to put you on the path towards those dreams and goals.

You will definitely experience some discomfort when you start to change the direction you were heading in. This is because our feelings, our personalities and everything else about us, are used to being who we are. We need to be ready for change. If we are ready for change in our lives, then we will be ready to see the opportunities around us.

Action

Once we start anticipating that opportunities will be coming our way, we need to act upon those opportunities. We all know the saying 'actions speak louder than words'. Well, it's so true when it comes to seizing opportunities.

There is no use getting to the end of your life and regretting the things you never did, or sitting discussing the opportunities that you saw in front of you but let go.

If I hadn't taken action when I saw the opportunity of starting my own business seven years ago, I might still be working for someone else, still miserable with the way my life was progressing. Who knows?

There are people all around who I call 'gunna guys'. We all know them, the people who are 'going to do this' or 'going to do that'. But they never do. These same people are the ones who, when success is happening to everyone around them, are the first to tell you they 'were going to do that years ago'. I can't stand that. They are attempting to take away your sense of achievement in order to make themselves more comfortable about their shortcomings. They try to bring everyone down to their level to make themselves feel equal, or even to give themselves a feeling of superiority.

You might be trying for a promotion at work; you might even want a better job. You need to act upon those desires for them to happen. If the job you want requires more qualifications than you have now, you need to achieve those qualifications before you will get the position. Achieving those qualifications will require action. You need to enrol in the courses that are required, attend the lectures and complete those courses.

If you have ever bought a house you will probably appreciate my next example.

My wife and I were looking to buy our first house. As I am not a patient person by anyone's standards, Vanessa was a bit concerned that this flaw of mine was going to make looking for a house a painful process for both of us. Everyone around us, our friends and families, had told us that it can takes ages to find that 'perfect house'.

We looked through the papers, on the Internet, and even went out every Saturday and picked up the latest homes magazines. The time had finally come: the first weekend of looking through the houses that had caught our eye.

We organised to meet the real estate agent at the first house that met our requirements. Nice, but not what we were looking for. The next house was just around the corner, and there were six more to look at that day.

No need. The second house was the one for us. It had absolutely everything we wanted and more. This was our opportunity. We had found our dream home, but we needed to act upon that dream and buy that house.

There were a few other people looking at the same time, so we hot-footed it back to the agent's office to put down a deposit. We needed to act fast, otherwise it might go to someone else. I am pleased to say that we have been in that house ever since and we still love it. Had we passed on that opportunity, we might still be looking, or we might have settled on something that wasn't as good.

Awareness

Another reason many of us miss opportunities is that we are not aware they're out there. We all need to stop once in a while and take time out to notice what is happening around us. Because our lives are so busy, and sometimes hectic, it is quite easy to miss those golden opportunities.

When Susan had initial success with her products, she was

ecstatic. She had achieved what she had set out to do. From a simple concept one day, in just over three months Susan had her products in three of the major retailers.

But then it all seemed to go pear-shaped. Sales of the products went really well, Susan had national exposure for her product lines and there was interest in ordering new designs. The biggest mistake Susan made, partly because it all happened so fast and with little effort in the first place, was not seeing or appreciating the new opportunities that were opening in front of her. All she saw was the money rolling in the door. She bought new furniture, moved house, spent money on this and that. Then the penny finally dropped. To capitalise on these potential new orders she needed more capital—but it was all gone.

Now remember, Susan started with nothing but an idea. She took the opportunity and made it work. She was in a great position to take the new opportunities on, but she was completely unaware they were there. When she finally realised what was right in front of her nose, it was too late. She had taken her eyes off the big picture and focused on the wrong things. Today, her business is worth less than when she started. What a waste of a great opportunity. Susan never appreciated what she had accomplished and in the end it all fell apart because she failed to change the way she was when she started.

Sir Winston Churchill once said, 'Continuous effort, not strength or intelligence, is the key to unlocking your potential.' With continuous effort comes opportunity. Over the years I have made some really good friends. One of my closest friends is Phillip Bamford. Phil is one of those guys you just like being around, as his thinking takes you to a higher platform in your own life. Phil is the leaseholder of a council-owned pool in my local area, which he took from a $300 000 business to a multimillion-dollar business in just three years. The key factor that sets Phil apart is that he is always looking for new opportunities.

Over the years Phil and I have discussed going into business together. We did try one venture, a website devoted to people having a place to complain about bad service, which we called <www.whinger.com.au>. Neither of us expected its unbelievable success (over 120 000 hits per week) and because both of us were so tied up in our other businesses at the time, we had to shut it down temporarily (otherwise we might have had people whingeing about whinger). We determined that the next time we tried something together we would both be able to devote the proper amount of time to it.

When I started out, the hardest thing to get my head around was the concept of cash flow. Cash flow is the biggest destroyer of small business. It isn't that there are no orders or sales coming in the door, it is that to grow your business you need to get more sales; to get more sales you need more stock; to get more stock you need more money to pay for it. At the same time you have to make sure you keep focused on the budgets you have set. Phil had also seen the dimensions of the problem. Always one to take advantage of an opportunity, Phil started talking about designing a programme which would help small businesses understand everything about their budgets, cash flow, incomes and outgoings. As this is the main bugbear of most small businesses, I could see the potential. Phil had no experience at all with computers, and no idea of what it would take to write an entire programme to do what we wanted it to do, but that didn't seem to bother him.

After many months of talking it through, and a lot of hours spent behind the computer, we launched 'The Business Cash Flow Manager' and our website <www.meltingpot.ozau.net>. We trialled the programme with a few select small businesses around our area and the response was overwhelming. We launched the product in July 2002 and sales went through the roof. The small business community couldn't wait to buy it. There have even been software companies, both in Australia and overseas, wanting to buy the rights from us. As a result of that success, we set out to provide small businesses with a range of software products that would make their lives just that little bit easier. Phil has always looked for opportunities. Most of the successes he has had over the years have come from taking the simplest ideas and turning them into reality.

Don't ever think that opportunities only come in big ways, with flashing signs attached. Some of the greatest success stories of our time have been people using simple ideas, taking the smallest of opportunities, and turning them into great accomplishments. Just have a look at the 'cat's eyes' that are on every road around the world. Simple idea, huge rewards. You see, opportunities will not always be sitting in front of your face. Sometimes you need to go and find them. You also need to understand that not every opportunity will turn out to be the one for you.

Over the years, I have been approached with ideas that to some might be 'the opportunity of a lifetime'. Sure, they might have been great ideas, but they weren't the right ones for me. I knew what I wanted to achieve, and I was positive that nothing would distract me along the way. You may be able to recall times when you have taken an opportunity that has either fallen on its face or taken you in a different direction to where you wanted to go.

Don't regret ... react

I do not believe in regrets. Focusing on regrets forces us to live in the past. As I just said, I have been offered many opportunities that I have chosen to pass on. Some of those opportunities have gone on to be major successes. Some have gone on to fall in a big heap. If I was to live my life regretting all the things that could have been, I would just be torturing myself and making everyone around me miserable. You will never see the opportunities in front of you if you are looking back and reflecting on what is behind you.

Some years ago Vanessa and I were having dinner with a successful and wealthy businessman, a true inspiration. He was one of the first people to take on the Attitude Inc.® brand in his stores, and we became good friends. Over the course of the dinner we talked about his success, including the ups and the downs.

He told us a story about how, many many years ago, in the United States on a business trip, he was offered the opportunity to start a franchise of hamburger takeaway stores in Australia. At that time the local corner hamburger shop was all the rage and he turned the offer down, thinking it wouldn't work in this country. No one would buy a hamburger from a restaurant, he told them.

That franchise was McDonald's. We were amazed at the way this man viewed missing this opportunity. Did he regret it? No. He decided years ago that he wouldn't regret, he would react instead. He reacted to missing this opportunity by finding another one. Had he spent the years that followed that decision, moaning and groaning about the 'what ifs', he would have subjected his thinking and actions to defeat. He understood that keeping his eyes fixed on the 'what will bes' was more important.

In late 2000, I was confronted with one of my biggest opportunities. Although I had licensed the Attitude Inc.® name and logo to a few different companies and products over the previous five years, I had really thought of licensing as only a small part of my business structure. I was approached by Licensing Essentials, my clothing manufacturers at the time, with the offer to license one of the clothing lines from me. This was not an easy decision, as the clothing line was my bread and butter. I had a big opportunity in front of me. Should I hang onto what was my 'security blanket', or should I take a risk and follow through with it? It took me two months to decide, as this was all about the future direction of my company. By the time I had made the decision to enter a new phase of the business, I had licensed more than ten new product lines.

Seizing this opportunity took me along a new and prosperous path. If I had not taken it, I might still be working the same old way, doing the same old things. Sure, my business would still have grown, but by being aware of the opportunity and acting on it, I was able to take a short cut to fulfilling one of my ultimate dreams. The lesson there was that the opportunity of a lifetime must be seized during the lifetime of the opportunity.

Today, Attitude Inc.® products grace the shelves of Big W, Rebel Sport and over 2000 independent stores across Australia, and are soon to be launched all over the world. As you can see, luck has nothing to do with it. When and if opportunities cross your path, make sure you make the most of them.

Many opportunities will not look like opportunities at first glance. Some may even start as a difficult situation or a problem. It is what you do to address the problem that could lead to an opportunity that will change the rest of your life.

WHY SETTLE FOR WHAT YOU'RE GIVEN IN LIFE? WHY NOT BE IN CHARGE OF WHAT LIFE HANDS OUT?

I heard someone say the other day, 'The more successful I get, the luckier I get.' It isn't luck you're getting. It is the more opportunities you are creating, simply by being aware of what is happening around you and grasping them.

Apply the 3 A's to your life and situations and see what will happen. Remember, you have to *anticipate* the opportunities, become *aware* that they are there, then *act* on them, before any good change will come about.

Try it. I dare you!

make it happen | 8 |

8

IT'S ALL ABOUT LUCK—
JUST ASK ANY LOSER

© Attitude Inc.®

A very important thing that many people don't realise when trying to achieve their dreams or reach their goals, is that only they are responsible for the outcome. No one else can be blamed for what happens in your life. Sure, curve balls will come across your path as you progress towards achieving your goals, but in the end you are the only one who can change their direction and hit them away. It is you who has to get off your butt and make your dreams happen!

We all need to make things happen in our lives, otherwise life will just happen around us. What I mean by that is you need to be the one who determines your progress towards your goals. Don't just sit there and wait for problems to happen, because then you will have to spend a whole heap of time fixing a situation you didn't need to get into in the first place. It is very easy to sit back and rely on things happening around you. But that is the easy way out and the results will be short lived.

Abraham Lincoln is a name you will probably recognise straight away. He was president of the United States in 1860. Let me share with you how Abraham Lincoln made his dream happen.

Abraham Lincoln was born in the backwoods of Kentucky in 1809. He worked as a flatboatman, a postmaster, a storekeeper, surveyor and rail-splitter before becoming a lawyer. All up, his formal education added up to about a year. Now when you think about it, that is not very long for someone who was going to achieve so much. He is a classic case of someone who dared to make it happen. He also dared to fail. Abraham Lincoln wasn't afraid of failing as long as he kept his eyes firmly fixed on his dream—as this list shows:

Failed in business in 1831.

Defeated in Illinois state legislature in 1832.

Failed in business in 1833.

Elected to Illinois state legislature in 1834

Had a nervous breakdown in 1836.

Defeated for Illinois House Speaker in 1838.

Defeated for nomination for Congress in 1843.

Elected to Congress in 1846.

Lost renomination for Congress in 1848.

Failed to be appointed as Commissioner of the General Lands Office in 1849.

Defeated for the United States Senate in 1854.

Defeated for nomination for Vice-President in 1856.

Defeated for the Senate again in 1858.

In 1860 he was elected as the sixteenth, and probably the most recognised, and one of the greatest presidents in American history.

Abraham Lincoln made his dream happen. It took years and a lot of setbacks, but through sheer determination and focus he reached his ultimate goal. He once said, 'To remain as I am is impossible; I must either die or be better.'

Are you determined to stay the same person you have always been? Do you want the same problems, issues and setbacks to be dictating how long it will take to reach those dreams and goals you have set? You need to make your dreams happen. Just like Abraham Lincoln, who went on to greatness, you need to push through those hurdles.

A friend of mine is constantly saying that he is 'nearly making it' in achieving his goals. Well, 'nearly making it' and 'making it' are miles apart.

While he is certainly having a go at trying to reach those goals, he is unfortunately not learning from his experiences. You won't always succeed at everything you try, but the only time you will truly fail is when you don't learn from the experience, and make the same mistakes over and over. I could 'nearly' win the lottery, but the person who actually does win it will be a little bit better off.

What is the use of having goals and dreams if you never get to achieve them? The whole point of dreaming is focusing on what you want to have in the future.

Dreams that are always too far from being fulfilled have the potential to turn into a personal nightmare and a constant source of frustration—unless you make a decision that you will make them happen no matter what. To achieve those dreams and goals you need the willpower to make them happen. You need to make a pact with yourself that no matter what interference comes your way, no matter what negative thinking starts up, you will stay focused on the end result.

How many times have you been to a movie or a sporting event and walked away afterwards all pumped up and ready to take on the world? And found yourself the next day back to the same old you, totally forgetting the feelings and emotions of the day before? We are all easily moved emotionally, for good or bad. The key is to harness that emotional feeling and turn it into an energy source. When we achieve something that brings us closer to our dreams and goals we feel on top of the world, nothing can stop us. It is a feeling you need to remember. That is how you want to feel all the time. Invincible.

When we hit a snag or run into a hurdle, we tend to feel defeated. Although it is a temporary setback, some of us keep that feeling in our memories. Having it there as a constant reminder is a negative energy source—and then we wonder why we are struggling to achieve. We become used to negative feelings, some of us even using them as a crutch and an excuse as to why we can't succeed in reaching our goals. Some people fail in their own heads before they even try anything. They only remember the negative.

I remember watching a State of Origin football match. As the Queensland team walked into the tunnel to go onto the field, they were pumped up. They knew that they had to win. One of the players yelled out at the top of his voice, 'Queenslander!' The raw emotion of that shout not only charged up the team, but also set the atmosphere in the watching crowd. The player had set the tone by shouting just one word, the benchmark.

What would have happened if by the time the team had reached the field they had lost that emotion and decided they couldn't be bothered? Their level of performance would have been affected and the crowd watching would have reacted negatively. Well, that didn't happen, and the game was played with determination and high energy.

Don't let your negative thoughts and emotions rule your direction. You need to be determined that you will make every action and thought count. You need to be determined that you are going to make it happen. The key is to not lose the feelings of either emotion or drive along the path to achieving your dreams.

DON'T LET TOTALLY IRRELEVANT ISSUES BLOCK YOUR VISION OF YOUR GOALS

Now I am on the speaking circuit I am normally booked in one of two categories: Motivational/Inspirational or Business Issues. I have shared the speaking stage with a lot of very motivational speakers and some very successful business people. It never ceases to amaze me how much excitement some of these speakers can produce in the listening audience. They have them jumping up and down, yelling out their dreams, even pledging total commitment to achieving all they want in their lives. That is fine, because as a speaker you can only leave the audience with your message; it is over to them to take the keys they have learnt about and apply them to their own lives.

Excitement is one thing, but I would rather have action in my life. Remember the saying 'actions speak louder than words'? Some people leave the seminars all revved up and ready to change their lives and their situations; they have even put a plan together in their heads on how exactly they will change their situation. But they don't put any action to the words they have heard, or the plan they have in their heads. Some will later complain that nothing has worked for them; they have forgotten the feelings that were stirred up in that conference or meeting and the actions they were 'going' to apply.

If you want to get fitter or you want to lose weight, it's not going to happen if you stay sitting in front of the television. You need to get up and go for a walk or go to the gym. I have been training at the gym now for many years and each week I see people start there with all the enthusiasm and energy in the world. They've decided they are going to lose those few kilos or tone their bodies if it's the last thing they do. They start with their goals in their sights but some of them, as soon as they realise that to achieve those goals will require a lot of hard work, discipline and a lot of action, seem to give up. They go back to accepting the old standards, just being content with the shape they were before. It is a cycle. They will continue to frustrate themselves until they decide to break that cycle and make their goals happen.

We seem to be motivated easily but the secret is to keep that fire of motivation alight within us, to carry that motivation as a guide and a tool to where we want to end up. I know someone who has job after job after job. The same issues surface in each job. He hasn't realised yet that, while it is good to talk about what he needs to address, the only time that he will overcome those issues is when he puts action behind those words.

My time at school was not a time of major achievement. I must admit I really didn't apply myself during my school years and now, looking back, I can understand how I would have annoyed almost any teacher I came in contact with. All I wanted was to be the class clown. The day I left school, one of my teachers stopped me at the gate and said, 'Mr Herald, you are a failure. It wouldn't surprise me if you end up either on the dole or dead.' Now, I could have listened to his words and lived my life by them but I decided to use them to my advantage. I knew that he was totally wrong about me, but I had to put actions to my thoughts. I decided that those words would be my motivation to prove him, and everyone else who had written me off, wrong.

Sure I stuffed up here and there as I went along, I made many mistakes, but not once did I ever reflect on those negative words and believe them. Ten years later, as I walked into a shop stocking my brand, the teacher who had given me his opinion of where my life was headed walked out. Recognising me, for some unknown reason he started into me again, asking if I was on the dole, if I had been in trouble. In a way he seemed shocked that I was still alive. There had been no love lost between the two of us at school but he seemed to have carried his resentment over the intervening years. I stood there and let him have his say; all I could do was smile. This didn't seem to impress him and he stormed off. You see, he was wearing one of my t-shirts! And he had no idea I was the owner of the brand. I found out later from the shop owner that he had bought a fair few of them because he 'really liked them and what they stood for'.

I made my dreams and future happen. I did not let someone's misguided opinions from ten years earlier rule my direction. What excess baggage are you hanging onto? You need to let some of it go. Opinions which are hurtful and wrong should never be the ruler of your direction.

Too many people brush off the positive inputs that come into their lives and focus only on the negative. Yet it is the positive inputs that are our source of energy and life. The minute that you let negativity get into your thinking, you are on the wrong track. Negativity leads you to question yourself and your goals too much; when we let this become a habit we tend to take the path of least resistance.

Don't look for trouble

Every time you look hard at the direction you are taking to reach your goals, you will undoubtedly find potential problems. But why go looking for trouble? Remember, when you look for a problem you will probably find one. All this does is take your focus off what you want to achieve and place it on what might stop you from achieving them. Negative thinking can keep us from reaching our goals and achieving our dreams. To make things happen in our lives we really need to address that thought process.

I know some people who are their own worst enemy when it comes to advancing their life. The dreams and goals they have set will always be in the distance as long as they have a negative opinion of themselves; their progress will be in the order of taking two steps forward and one step backward, at best.

DARE TO DREAM

When I left school I had many dreams. Big ones, medium ones and small ones. The big dreams were so big that there was no point dwelling on them. Even then, I knew that one day, if I put my life into perspective and worked my way through the small dreams, then onto the medium dreams, I was sure to end up working on my big dreams. Don't make the mistake of aiming only at your biggest dreams. They require a lot of time, effort and experience. It is the experience that we get from achieving our smaller goals and dreams that becomes useful when tackling our bigger ones.

I have met many people who have given up on reaching their goals and their dreams simply because they aimed too high to start with. It is the little goals, and the sense of accomplishment that you get when you fulfil and reach them, that will help you on your journey towards the bigger ones. You have to learn from the mistakes you make along the way. Those lessons will prove invaluable in the future with your other goals.

The only way I would ever achieve any of my dreams was to start making my opportunities happen. I was not prepared to sit back, take what came to me and react accordingly. The feeling of success and accomplishment you get when you are finally standing in front of your goal and dream really is worth the effort.

My best mate, Marty, was always talking about owning his own crane business. Over the years he worked for numerous crane companies, first as a dogman, eventually as the driver of these huge machines. One day Marty decided that he was going to make his dream a reality. He took a risk and bought his own crane.

He now runs a very successful business, but unless he had decided one day that it was now or never, he would still be just dreaming about what could be. You need to be the captain steering your own ship. You have to make things happen. You need what I call a 'whatever it takes' attitude. You need to set a standard in your life that you will not accept anything but achieving your goals and dreams.

As I have said several times—and it's worth repeating—it is what you focus on that will ultimately be where you end up. Don't accept negativity around you; don't accept that you may fail along the way. Do accept that you are going to do whatever it takes, for however long it takes, to get there.

Impatience gets you nowhere

Through speaking at conferences I find myself talking to a lot of people who are terribly frustrated because they know where they want to end up in life but haven't got there yet. They have become impatient and their impatience has got the better of them; they are ready to give up because they are living a life of frustration. I understand their feelings; I am a very impatient person, I want everything and I want it now, but I have learnt that some things will, and need to, take some time.

In this era of instant coffee, instant meals and drive-through takeaway, we have become used to getting everything quickly. But reaching our goals takes time. I think that's a good thing, though, because it forces us to evaluate the processes we need to take. You can make it happen, but it won't happen overnight, as they say in an ad on television. You need to understand and accept that it may be a long haul. It may take a long time. Anything that comes too quickly normally isn't appreciated as much as something you had to spend time and effort to get.

I began Attitude Inc.® with the biggest plans under the sun, but to start off I had to print those first four t-shirts, then find someone to buy them, then repeat the process over and over until I could get to my big dreams. That process took a long time. Some people say that I have done it very quickly—but when it's you, it seems like a lifetime. The lessons that you learn along the way are invaluable.

As I said at the beginning of this chapter, you are the only person who will make it possible to reach your dreams or destiny. You are the one who will go through trials and tests of your character. You are the one who will handle the disappointments. Ultimately it is you who will benefit from the hard work and persistence. But are *you* ready for all that lies ahead in your life and what it may bring? If you say 'no' at this point, put the book down and give yourself an uppercut!

Remember, it is hard work and persistence that makes success happen. Luck plays no part in success and pursuing your dreams. The people who constantly whinge that you are just 'lucky' are the ones who never do anything to better themselves, or expect everyone else to get them through life.

When someone does give them a hand or some good advice, they act as if they've done everything themselves, and never show any appreciation. They never realise that it requires a lot of effort to be successful. No matter what you tell some of these people, they will always pass off your success, and that of others, as luck.

YOU WILL NEVER BE ABLE TO PLEASE EVERYONE ALL OF THE TIME, SO DON'T TRY

I learnt this very quickly. Most of those around you will be right behind you and supportive at the start. They will think that it is great that you want a different job, direction or challenge. As you start moving ahead and closer to your goals, however, they may start telling you that you need to 'slow down a bit', 'we never get to see you any more'. What you have done is set a new standard for yourself. If this threatens people around you it may be because you are making them see that they have let go of their original dreams, that maybe they need to get off their butts and take control of their lives. If this happens, remember, you need to keep yourself happy first. Don't be pulled down to their level; if anything, you need to pull them up to yours. If you can't, then re-evaluate whether they are worth having around, feeding you negative inputs. It might sound harsh, but I don't want to get to the end of my life knowing that I 'could' have achieved my goals and dreams, but didn't because I listened to others around me!

My wife Vanessa has been at home for the first year of our

younger daughter's life. Vanessa's ultimate dream in life was to be a stay-at-home mum, to be there for our girls all the time.

At the time of writing, Brooke was 13 months old and Vanessa was finding that she had a fair bit of spare time on her hands. One day over coffee she started to share her frustration at wanting to do something but not knowing what. We talked about her strengths and she went away and thought about it herself. She came back a few hours later with a list of new goals and dreams.

The list was great, but of course Vanessa knew things wouldn't just happen by themselves. She understands the principle of making things happen. Within a week she had set up her new business and was firing on all cylinders. She has had to juggle things around a bit, but because she now has a means of fulfilling her dreams, she has been able to master what needs to be done. Once you are focused and committed, achieving your goals and dreams gets a bit easier. It is the process of getting started that seems to put a lot of us off the whole idea.

Whether you end up achieving your dreams and goals will be a direct result of the choices you make along the way. We all have choices in life. Do you get into your car and drive after having a big night out? Do you take that course that will give you better opportunities with employment? Do you apply the ideas in this book to your life, and maybe even get back on your path towards your goals? We are confronted with choices every day. It is the direction you take with that choice that will eventually take you down a path. Which path and what direction is up to you.

We all learn that we are faced with choices from an early age. The other day Brooke came into my office. She started to pull the papers from my waste bin.

I said 'no' and she stopped. A couple of minutes later she came back. I kept going about my work. When I realised that I hadn't heard boo from her for a couple of minutes, I looked over to my bin and there she was, about to reach for the papers again. She looked around to see if I was watching. As soon as she realised I was, she stopped and walked out of the room, taking a peek around the corner to check whether I was still watching.

She understood, even at her young age, that she had a choice to make. Touch the bin and get into trouble or leave it alone as she was told.

It amazes me the number of people who make the same wrong choices time after time. They never seem to learn from the negative outcomes, they still go down the same path. To make anything happen in our lives we need to make as many right choices as we can. You won't get it right all the time, but at least you are giving it a go. My sister-in-law was recently offered what seemed a great job which would have got her to one of her dreams a lot quicker than her current one. After some thought she took the job. She had made a choice.

A few months later, the job proved to be lacking in a lot of areas, and she found that in reality she was going in the opposite direction from her goals and dreams. She was working on average 60 hours each week running someone else's business, but being paid for only 38 hours. She now had another choice: stay there or move on. She chose the latter option. It wasn't that she didn't like or want the work, it was that she knew that while she had been promised one thing, the reality was that it would never be.

You will be faced with choices all the time. One key to achieving your dreams and goals is to understand that you will make some bad choices sometimes, but you don't need to get hung up over them. Just move on.

Another principle behind making things happen in our lives is doing what's not expected. Too often we just do our jobs to the minimum standard our job description prescribes. We shut our shops right on 5.30 pm because that is our closing time. We do just what our job description states we should do, we operate within set expectations. It is the things you do that go beyond what you and others around you expect that will ultimately be a factor in the timing of your success.

We set expectations on those around us; we even set our own expectations. You need to push up those expectations from within your thinking. As long as you operate by set expectations, you are essentially limiting yourself to them.

Start by setting new expectations for yourself on a daily basis. If month by month, year by year, you are still no closer to achieving your goals and dreams, then start questioning if it is because you are only operating to minimum expectations.

Let me give you an example how some people apply this principle. You may work in a large organisation. You have been there for years doing your job well. You never turn up late, you stay until knock-off time, you may even participate in the staff raffle. Someone new starts working there and within no time they have got that promotion and seem to be the 'favourite'. You might find that the reason this person has made such an impact is that they are doing the unexpected. They are there 30 minutes before they are supposed to be, they leave when the work is finished, no matter what the time, they may even be doing courses to better their qualifications.

Unfortunately, many people out there are very good at knocking someone who is going beyond the norm. But it is those of us who go that extra distance who in the end will prosper and achieve our goals.

I am constantly amused by the number of people who decide to quit their jobs and work for themselves because they are never appreciated in their current employment and are sick and tired of putting in all those extra hours. They think that by working for themselves they will do better. So off they go into the big world of being self-employed. The problem with that scenario is if they approach their new business with only the same level of effort, commitment and expectation that they had previously, they will still have the same issues. Owning and running a business requires thinking outside the square. There is no knock-off time, because you now are the business.

If you do only what you think is expected, you will eventually fall short. The concept of always doing what isn't expected is the tool that will grow you, in employment or your own business. Unfortunately a lot of business owners never realise this fact, and as a result are miserable in their chosen path.

It is up to you to make your dreams and goals happen. Don't copy anyone else, because their life and direction is exactly that. Theirs. Determine today that you are going to do whatever it takes to make your life happen. Then sit back and hold on for the ride.

IN THE END IT'S ALL A MATTER OF ATTITUDE

www.justinherald.com